Take &Rea

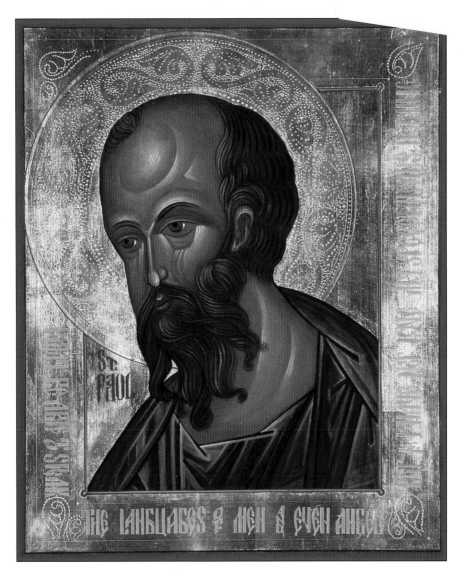

The Letter to
the Romans

Adrian Graffy

Published in 2012 by Alive Publishing Ltd.
Graphic House, 124 City Road, Stoke on Trent, ST4 2PH.
Tel: +44 (0) 1782 745600   Fax: +44 (0) 1782 745500
www.alivepublishing.co.uk

©2012 Alive Publishing
British Library Catalogue-in-Publication Data.
A catalogue record for this book is available from the British Library.

ISBN 978-1-906278-16-8

Front cover and image on previous page: St Paul by Marek Czarnecki, based on the famous fifteenth-
century prototype by Russian iconographer Saint Andrei Rublev.

Contents

Editor's Foreword

One of the features of the Church of today is the rediscovery of the Bible. In the years since the Second Vatican Council this thirst for the Scriptures has become stronger and stronger. The desire for a deeper engagement with the Bible is clear from the enormous popularity of publications such as *Walk with Me* and *Bible Alive*.

Take and Read is designed to assist people in their need to understand the Bible more deeply. The series has been developed as a follow-up to the document *The Gift of Scripture*, which was produced in 2005 by the Bishops of England and Wales, and of Scotland, to mark the 40th anniversary of the Council document on Divine Revelation, *Dei Verbum*.

The story of the conversion of Saint Augustine to the Catholic faith inspired the title of the series. He recounts in his 'Confessions' how he heard a voice calling to him with the words *Tolle, lege* 'Take and Read'. At that moment he picked up the New Testament and read the first chapter his eyes fell upon, from the Letter to the Romans. His conversion was assured.

These books are a major new resource for prayerful reading of the Scriptures both for groups and for individuals. Passages from the Scriptures are accompanied by commentary, quotations from the Fathers and from Church documents, Christian art and inspiring photographs, as well as suggestions for prayer and reflection.

It is a great pleasure to acknowledge the work of those who helped develop this series. Representatives from dioceses throughout Britain worked on the preparatory stages. Particular thanks should go to Anne White, Anne Dixon and Sister Vicky Hummel. I record my gratitude to the authors who have collaborated with me in working on the series. After the initial books on the four gospels we are now turning our attention to other books of the New Testament. I am particularly grateful for the support of Mike Conway of *Alive Publishing*, who readily agreed to publish the *Take and Read* series.

Take and Read will help you to delve more deeply into the Scriptures, to understand them better, and to pray with the Scriptures. *Take and Read* will assist you in *lectio divina,* that prayerful reading of Scripture which has always been central to the life of the Church.

Fr Adrian Graffy

Introduction to Romans

The Dominican biblical scholar, Marie-Joseph Lagrange, who in 1890 founded the *Ecole Biblique* in Jerusalem, said this about reading the Letter to the Romans: 'The first contact with Romans was overwhelming.' Decades later the renowned Jesuit New Testament scholar Joseph Fitzmyer recalled Lagrange's words and wrote: 'Every contact with Romans is overwhelming.' Paul is not easy.

In the Second Letter of Peter we read: 'There are some things in Paul's letters hard to understand, which the ignorant and unstable twist to their own destruction, as they do the other scriptures. You, therefore, beloved, since you are forewarned, beware that you are not carried away with the error of the lawless and lose your own stability' (3:16-17). It has long been known that Paul is not easy.

Nevertheless, the Letter to the Romans is the most worthwhile of all Paul's letters, presenting as it does in all its fullness 'the Gospel of Paul', not a gospel invented by him, but an inspired explanation of the full meaning of Christ's death and resurrection.

It is hoped that this volume will encourage Christians of different communities to become familiar with this letter. The controversies of the Reformation led to conflicting interpretations, but ecumenical dialogue is healing such differences.

Romans will reward the efforts we make to understand it. It expresses the heart of the good news in a way no other New Testament document does. 'He died for our sins, and rose again for our justification' (4:25). 'There is no condemnation for those who are in Christ Jesus' (8:1). 'The gospel is the power of God for salvation to everyone who has faith' (1:16).

In a sermon on a text of Romans, Blessed John Henry Newman wrote: 'Nothing can deprive us of our hope of heaven. But on the other hand how little we understand our privileges; how little we understand the words of the sacred writers about them. May God enlighten our eyes to see what the privileges are.' *(Faith and Prejudice 109)*

Opposite: St Paul by El Greco.

Paul and his Gospel

Hear the Word of God

Romans 1:1-17

[1] Paul, a servant of Jesus Christ, called to be an apostle, set apart for the gospel of God, [2] which he promised beforehand through his prophets in the holy scriptures, [3] the gospel concerning his Son, who was descended from David according to the flesh [4] and was declared to be Son of God with power according to the spirit of holiness by resurrection from the dead, Jesus Christ our Lord, [5] through whom we have received grace and apostleship to bring about the obedience of faith among all the Gentiles for the sake of his name, [6] including yourselves who are called to belong to Jesus Christ, [7] To all God's beloved in Rome, who are called to be saints:

Grace to you and peace from God our Father and the Lord Jesus Christ.

[8] First, I thank my God through Jesus Christ for all of you, because your faith is proclaimed throughout the world. [9] For God, whom I serve with my spirit by announcing the gospel of his Son, is my witness that without ceasing I remember you always in my prayers, [10] asking that by God's will I may somehow at last succeed in coming to you. [11] For I am longing to see you so that I may share with you some spiritual gift to strengthen you— [12] or rather so that we may be mutually encouraged by each other's faith, both yours and mine. [13] I want you to know, brothers and sisters, that I have often intended to come to you (but thus far have been prevented), in order that I may reap some harvest among you as I have among the rest of the Gentiles. [14] I am a debtor both to Greeks and to barbarians, both to the wise and to the foolish [15]— hence my eagerness to proclaim the gospel to you also who are in Rome.

[16] For I am not ashamed of the gospel; it is the power of God for salvation to everyone who has faith, to the Jew first and also to the Greek. [17] For in it the righteousness of God is revealed through faith for faith; as it is written, 'The one who is righteous will live by faith.'

Understand the Word of God

This session will explore:

- ❖ Paul's understanding of his call
- ❖ his desire to visit Rome
- ❖ the theme of the letter

Setting in the Letter

These are the opening verses of the letter. Paul's greeting in the first sentence is extremely long and covers the first seven verses. After this initial greeting comes the thanksgiving in verses 8-15. Our passage ends with verses 16-17 which are the start of the first doctrinal section of the letter, which runs from 1:16 to 4:25.

Papyrus 10 is an early copy of part of the New Testament content in Greek. It is a papyrus manuscript of the Epistle to the Romans, dating paleographically to the early 4th century.

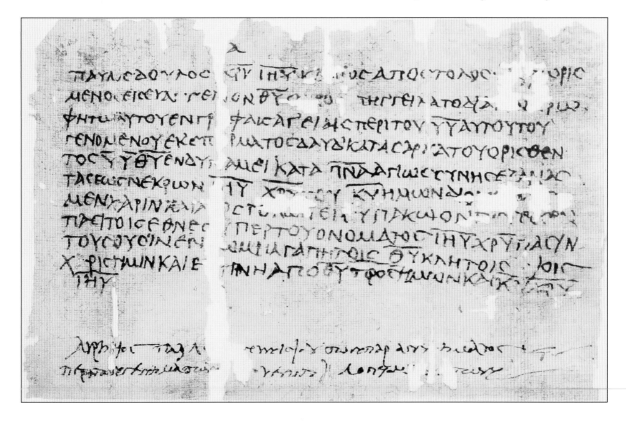

The Acts of the Apostles (23:26) records a letter from the Roman tribune in Jerusalem to the governor Felix. It begins:

Claudius Lysias to his Excellency the governor Felix, greetings!

The Books of Maccabees contain reports of several letters. The letter sent by the Jews to their potential allies the Spartans is reported in 1 Maccabees 12. It begins as follows:

The high priest Jonathan, the senate of the nation, the priests, and the rest of the Jewish people to their brothers the Spartans, greetings.

What Kind of Text?

Letters in Paul's day began with an opening, or prescript, which had a clear format. Our modern letters begin 'Dear So-and so' and conclude with the signing-off of the writer. Ancient papyrus letters began with the name of the writer. This is the format Paul follows. The essence of the opening in Romans is 'Paul, to the people in Rome, grace and peace.' But Paul has considerably expanded this basic opening.

There is a simpler opening at the beginning of the first letter to the Thessalonians: 'Paul, Silvanus, and Timothy, to the church of the Thessalonians in God the Father and the Lord Jesus Christ: Grace to you and peace.'

The opening in Romans is the longest opening in any letter of Paul, due to the profession of faith which Paul inserts after saying he is 'set apart for the gospel of God'.

There follows an extended thanksgiving in verses 8-15. The announcement of the main theme of the letter comes in verses 16-17.

Commentary: verse by verse reading

Initial Greeting

v.1 Paul presents himself in three ways. Firstly, he is 'a slave of Christ Jesus' (Greek *doulos Christou Iesou)*. In Philippians 1:1 Paul and Timothy are described as 'slaves of Christ Jesus'. In Titus 1:1 Paul is 'a slave of God' (Greek *doulos theou*).

Secondly, he is 'called to be an apostle' (Greek *kletos apostolos*), one who is sent. Paul is insistent that he is an apostle even though he was not associated with Jesus in his ministry and is not one of the Twelve. In 1 Corinthians 15:9 he says: 'I am the least of the apostles… because I persecuted the church of God'. Galatians 1:1 expands on his call to be an apostle: 'an apostle – sent neither by human commission nor from human authorities, but through Jesus Christ and God the Father, who raised him from the dead'.

A literal translation of the Greek of Galatians 1:1 is much briefer: an apostle not from men or through a man, but through Jesus Christ and God the Father.

Thirdly, Paul is 'set apart (Greek *aphorismenos*) for the gospel of God'. Paul speaks in similar terms in Galatians 1:15: 'God set me apart before I was born'. In Acts 13:2 the voice of the Holy Spirit is heard setting Barnabas and Paul apart for a particular mission: 'Set apart for me Barnabas and Saul for the work to which I have called them.' This is the instigation for the first missionary journey of Barnabas and Paul.

This special choosing by God is similar to the choosing of the prophets, such as Jeremiah, or the calling of the Servant of the Lord in Second Isaiah:

Jeremiah 1:5 'Before I formed you in the womb I knew you, and before you were born I consecrated you.'

Isaiah 49:1 'The Lord called me before I was born, while I was in my mother's womb he named me.'

Paul is insistent that he proclaims the 'gospel' (Greek *euaggelion*). The original meaning of 'good news' is not the written accounts of the four evangelists, but the proclamation of the message of the death and resurrection of Jesus. Here Paul calls it 'the gospel of God', in verse 9 'the gospel of his son', in verse 16 simply 'the gospel' and in 16:25 he even calls it 'my gospel'.

The phrase 'the gospel of God', found repeatedly in Paul's letters, is also found in:

Mark 1:14 Jesus came to Galilee, proclaiming the gospel of God.

1 Peter 4:17 What will be the end for those who do not obey the gospel of God?

v.2 The start of the Letter to the Hebrews also suggests that the gospel was prepared for by the prophets: 'Long ago God spoke to our ancestors in many and various ways by the prophets.' The link between the gospel and the Jewish Scriptures is presented in many different ways by the New Testament writers.

Paul insists that God's plan is being realised. The Scriptures prepared the way for the 'righteousness' of God. Romans 3:21 reads: 'But now, apart from law, the righteousness of God has been disclosed, and is attested by the law and the prophets.' In Romans 16:25-27 Paul will speak of the mystery kept secret, but now disclosed and made known.

v.3 The human condition of Jesus is now considered. He 'came into being according to the flesh' by being descended from David. This recalls the magnificent line in John's Prologue: 'And the Word became flesh' (*John 1:14*). The Greek words are similar.

v.4 The second description of the Son is more complex. Jesus was 'declared Son of God with power according to the spirit of holiness by resurrection from the dead'. Jesus was 'established in power' as a consequence of his death and resurrection. The one who was born of David's line 'according to the flesh' is now revealed as Son of God and risen Saviour 'according to the spirit'.

St Augustine of Hippo teaches:

Paul had to oppose the unbelief of those who accept our Lord Jesus Christ only according to the man whom he put on but do not understand his divinity, which sets him apart from every creature.

(Rudimentary Exposition of the Epistle to the Romans 4)

In verses 3-4 Paul implies that Jesus Christ is true man, of the line of David, and true God. His eternal divine sonship has been made known in power through the resurrection. Philippians 2:6-11 similarly speaks of his divine status, his human self-emptying (Greek *kenosis*), and his establishment as 'Lord'. The Letter to the Romans, written about 57 AD, shows a profound grasp of the mystery of Christ. Verse 4 ends by proclaiming him as 'Jesus Christ our Lord'.

v.5 The gifts of Jesus are grace (Greek *charis*) and apostleship (Greek *apostole*), best understood as 'the grace of apostleship'. *Charis* is the Greek word for the Hebrew concepts of God's *hesed* and *hen*, God's constant loving mercy. It is the first element in the greeting in verse 7. *Apostole* is found here and in two other texts in Paul.

In 1 Corinthians 9:1-2 Paul is defending his status. In verse 1 he asks, 'Am I not an apostle?' and in verse 2 he continues, 'If I am not an apostle to others, at least I am to you; for you are the seal of my apostleship in the Lord.' In Galatians 2:8 we read: 'For the one who worked through Peter for the apostleship of the circumcision also worked through me (in sending me) to the Gentiles.' Paul implies equal status with Peter. While Peter was sent to the Jews, Paul is 'the apostle of the Gentiles' (*Romans 11:13*).

The phrase 'the obedience of faith' will be found again at the end of the letter (16:26). Faith (Greek *pistis*) is mentioned for the first time in the letter. The whole aim of the preaching is to bring Gentiles to faith (as well as affirming faith among the Jews). Paul's consciousness of his mission to the Gentiles, to the nations of the earth, was fed particularly by the prophets, such as the Second Isaiah, who spoke of the coming to faith of the nations.

v.6 Even though Paul seems to be addressing Gentiles here, the church of Rome was in fact made up of both Jews and Gentiles. Christianity seems to have reached Rome in the early 40s AD.

Jews were expelled from Rome by the emperor Claudius in 49 AD, returning at his death in 54. The Roman historian Suetonius suggests that the Jews were expelled because of 'disturbances about Christ'. This seems to refer to differences among the Jews in Rome about whether Jesus was the Messiah. When Paul writes his letter the church is once again a church of Jews and Gentiles. Earlier, when he was in Corinth, Paul had lodged with Aquila and Priscilla, a Jewish Christian couple who had recently arrived from Italy 'because Claudius had ordered all the Jews to leave Rome' (Acts 18:2).

Imperial portrait of Roman emperor Claudius (10 BC–54 AD).

v.7 Paul's greeting is of 'grace and peace'. Grace (Greek *charis*) is the loving mercy of the God of the Jews. Peace (Greek *eirene*) is the typical Jewish greeting of *shalom*, which has the broad meaning of things being as God would wish. These gifts come from God our Father and the Lord Jesus Christ. Jesus as *kyrios* is equal to the Father, as in verse 4.

Thanksgiving

1 Thessalonians 1:2-3 We always give thanks to God for all of you and mention you in our prayers, constantly remembering before our God and Father your work of faith and labour of love and steadfastness of hope in our Lord Jesus Christ.

v.8 There is often a thanksgiving at the beginning of a letter. In 1 Thessalonians 1:2-3 Paul thanks God for the faith, hope and love of the Thessalonians. In the Letter to the Galatians there is no thanksgiving, because Paul is reprimanding them for turning to 'another gospel', the gospel of works (*Galatians 1:6-9*). Here Paul thanks God for the faith of the Romans. Is this because 'faith' is such an important concept in the letter? Or is it because he knows very little about them, except that they are Christians? Is it an exaggeration to say that their faith is 'proclaimed throughout the world'?

v.9 Paul prays for the Roman church. He uses the same phrase in 1 Thessalonians 1:2, when Paul, Silvanus and Timothy 'make memory' of the Thessalonians.

v.10 He prays that he may be able to visit them. He says 'at last', implying that he has long wished to visit them. Such a journey will be made 'by God's will'. Paul speaks of going to Corinth 'if the Lord wills' in 1 Corinthians 4:19. The phrase 'God willing' (Greek *tou theou thelontos*) is common in papyrus letters of the time.

1 Thessalonians 3:6 Timothy has told us also that you always remember us kindly and long to see us – just as we long to see you.

v.11 Paul says he is longing to see them. A similar expression is found in 1 Thessalonians 3:6 of the local church's desire to see Paul and his desire to see them. Paul wishes to share 'some spiritual gift'. It is unclear what he means. Is it the letter, or simply his presence with them?

v.12 The phrase 'or rather', which is literally 'that is' (Greek *touto de estin*), introduces a qualification of a previous statement. There is an abrupt change here as Paul suggests that the Roman Christians may have spiritual gifts for him. He is seeking to ensure good relations with them. This is the only community to whom he writes which was not founded by Paul, and he is understandably nervous.

v.13 Paul has often planned to visit Rome but he has been prevented, seemingly by his missionary activity. In Romans chapter 15 he refers to his missionary work from Jerusalem and as far around the Mediterranean as Illyricum, the area north of Macedonia. He explains that it is his policy only to go to places where the Good News has not yet been preached. His intention is to call at Rome on his way to Spain. In talking here of 'reaping a harvest' he seems once more to be putting himself in charge.

v.14 Paul sees it as his duty, as apostle of the Gentiles (*Romans 11:13*), to preach to them too. He 'owes' the gospel to them. 'Greeks' are not only those who live in the area of Greece but all those who speak Greek, for the Greek language had spread around the eastern Mediterranean after the conquests of Alexander the Great (died 323 BC). The 'barbarians' (Greek *barbaroi*, from the unintelligibility of their languages) are those who do not know Greek, and do not share Hellenistic culture. Perhaps Paul is expecting to encounter such barbarians in Spain. What does Paul mean by the 'wise' and the 'foolish'? Maybe this is simply another way, like 'Gentiles and barbarians', of referring to all people.

v.15 Paul reiterates his desire to 'bring the gospel' to them. Once again there is some ambiguity. Have they not already received it? This verse may also refer to what he is doing in writing the letter, explaining the 'gospel of God'. Verse 16 goes straight in to explaining what the gospel is.

Texts about Paul's plans to go to Spain:

Romans 15:23-24 But now, with no further place for me in these regions, I desire, as I have for many years, to come to you when I go to Spain. For I do hope to see you on my journey and to be sent on by you, once I have enjoyed your company for a little while.

Romoans 15:28-29 I will set out by way of you to Spain; and I know that when I come to you, I will come in the fulness of the blessing of Christ.

According to Acts 28:1-2 Paul encounters 'barbarians' on the island of Malta:

After we had reached safety, we then learned that the island was called Malta. The natives (Greek barbaroi) showed us unusual kindness.

The Theme of the Letter

v.16 Paul is 'not ashamed' of the gospel. Why would he be ashamed? Paul had understood that if salvation came through faith in Jesus Christ then it did not come through obedience to the law. This understanding of the gospel had been attacked by Christian converts from Judaism who maintained that all Christians, whether Jew or Gentile, should abide by the Jewish law.

Paul keeps to the gospel as he understands it. He describes the gospel as 'the power of God'.

In 1 Corinthians 1:18 he refers to 'the message of the cross' (logos tou staurou) as 'the power of God', and in 1 Corinthians 1:24 he calls Christ 'the power and the wisdom of God'. The power of God is revealed in the gospel of the cross of Christ.

It is Christ who brings 'salvation'. The word 'salvation' (Greek *soteria*) is used here for the first time in the letter. Romans 5:9 explains: 'Now that we have been justified by his blood, we will be saved through him from the wrath of God.' The concept of salvation has its origins in the Old Testament. The first of all acts of salvation of God for Israel was the Exodus. The prophets, such as the Second Isaiah, speak of a future salvation. New Testament writers such as St Paul drew on a rich heritage when they spoke of salvation in Christ.

Faith, which is a dominant theme in verses 16-17, means here a radical trust in the goodness of God shown in Christ Jesus. The Jews are the first recipients of the gospel, but the Greeks are also invited to have faith, as indeed are all people. Paul will explain at greater length how the Jews fit in to God's plan in Romans 9-11.

v.17 Paul now introduces the concept which is central to the letter, and particularly to the first doctrinal part (*1:16-4:25*), the 'righteousness' of God. He says that, in the gospel, this righteousness is being revealed (Greek *apokaluptetai*). There is a sense here of an apocalyptic revelation, a revelation of the end time.

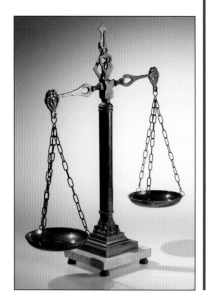

The righteousness or justice (Greek *dikaiosune*) of God contrasts with the anger (Greek *orge*) of God in verse 18. The phrase 'righteousness of God' is found seven times in Romans and only in 2 Corinthians 5:21 elsewhere in Paul's writings. It is most frequent in Romans 3:21-26. It refers to God's way of exercising justice.

In the Old Testament the Hebrew word for righteousness is *sedaqah* and it is clearly an attribute or quality of God. In the prophets particularly God exercises righteousness in favour of the sinful, a righteousness which brings mercy and forgiveness. In Isaiah 46:13 God brings righteousness and salvation. In Paul's preaching it is Christ's action which makes God's righteousness accessible.

In the Latin Vulgate translation the Greek word dikaiosune *is translated as* justitia, *thus 'justice' in English. 'Justice' is understood as the process by which sin is punished, what is called retributive justice. This conflicts with the sense Paul has in mind, where God's saving forgiveness is uppermost.*

'Through faith for faith'. This is a difficult phrase, which might mean that the righteousness of God is experienced by those who have faith, and in turn builds faith up. Paul then gives the first of many Old Testament quotations. It is from Habakkuk 2:4, 'The righteous person will live by faith.' Paul draws on the prophets for his understanding of Christ.

Paul's point is that the righteous person will live because of faith in the saving work of Jesus. 'Justification by faith' speaks of the power of Christ to save us, for we cannot save ourselves. But faith always implies something more than faith alone, as Paul himself makes clear in Galatians 5:6: 'the only thing that counts is faith working through love.'

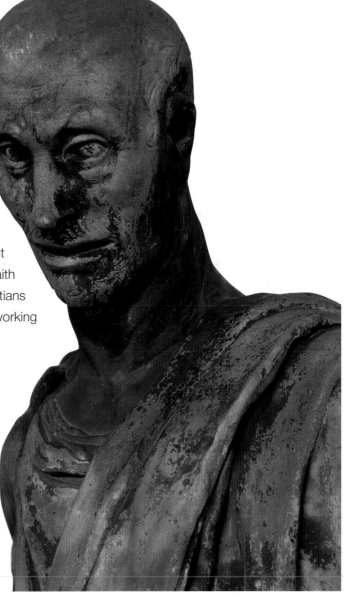

Habakkuk by Donatello.

The Dream of St Joseph by
Rembrandt.

The Word Lives On

The Letter to the Romans enjoys four whole weeks (weeks 28 to 31)
of the ferial lectionary, in Year 1. Romans 1:1-7 is read on the Monday
of the 28th week and a passage beginning with Romans 1:16 on the
Tuesday.

Romans 1:1-7 is also read in Year A on the Fourth Sunday of Advent,
when it accompanies the gospel of the message of the angel to
'Joseph, son of David' in Matthew 1:18-24. Verse 3 of the Romans
text describes the Son of God as 'descended from David according
to the flesh'.

Live the Word of God

Listen once more to the reading.

Suggestions for reflection and prayer

Paul is fiercely proud of his role as apostle.

❖ How convinced am I that God sends me too to proclaim the good news?

Paul wants to give, but he is aware also of receiving.

❖ How do I achieve a balance in giving and receiving?

Paul is determined to continue preaching in Rome and beyond.

❖ Do I desire to bring the message of faith to people who do not know or understand it?

The good news of salvation in Christ is his fundamental belief.

❖ Do I believe that I am saved by faith in Jesus Christ, and that faith should be lived out in love?

Christians have long disputed what 'justification by faith' means. After the Reformation the followers of Martin Luther stressed God's role in the process of justification, while Catholic reaction stressed human collaboration with God's grace. In 1999 a Joint Declaration on Justification was made by the Catholic Church and the World Lutheran Federation, which demonstrated a new consensus. It reads: Justification is the forgiveness of sins, liberation from the dominating power of sin and death and from the curse of the law. It is acceptance into communion with God: already now, but then fully in God's coming kingdom. It unites with Christ and with his death and resurrection. It occurs in the reception of the Holy Spirit in baptism and incorporation into the one body. All this is from God alone, for Christ's sake, by grace, through faith in 'the gospel of God's Son'. (paragraph 11)

Martin Luther.

The missionary journeys of St Paul.

Justification by Faith

Hear the Word of God

Romans 3:21–4:5

[21] But now, irrespective of law, the righteousness of God has been disclosed, and is attested by the law and the prophets, [22] the righteousness of God through faith in Jesus Christ for all who believe. For there is no distinction, [23] since all have sinned and fall short of the glory of God; [24] they are now justified by his grace as a gift, through the redemption that is in Christ Jesus, [25] whom God put forward as a sacrifice of atonement by his blood, effective through faith. He did this to show his righteousness, because in his divine forbearance he had passed over the sins previously committed; [26] it was to prove at the present time that he himself is righteous and that he justifies the one who has faith in Jesus.

[27] Then what becomes of boasting? It is excluded. By what law? By that of works? No, but by the law of faith. [28] For we hold that a person is justified by faith apart from works prescribed by the law. [29] Or is God the God of Jews only? Is he not the God of Gentiles also? Yes, of Gentiles also, [30] since God is one; and he will justify the circumcised on the ground of faith and the uncircumcised through that same faith. [31] Do we then overthrow the law by this faith? By no means! On the contrary, we uphold the law.

[4:1] What then are we to say was gained by Abraham, our ancestor according to the flesh? [2] For if Abraham was justified by works, he has something to boast about, but not before God. [3] For what does the scripture say? 'Abraham believed God, and it was reckoned to him as righteousness.' [4] Now to one who works, wages are not reckoned as a gift but as something due. [5] But to one who without works trusts him who justifies the ungodly, such faith is reckoned as righteousness.

Opposite: Melchisedek offering bread and wine to Abraham, nave mosaic from the church of Sta. Maria Maggiore in Rome, c. 432-440 A.D.

Understand the Word of God

This session will explore:

- ❖ the meaning of God's righteousness
- ❖ the justification of the sinner
- ❖ the role of faith
- ❖ the example of Abraham

Setting in the Letter

The theme of the righteousness or justice (Greek *dikaiosune*) of God was announced by Paul in 1:16-17. This theme dominates the letter until 4:25. In Paul's preaching Christ brings justification and salvation to those who have faith.

In 1:18-3:20 Paul illustrates how people behave without the gospel. He refers to the idolatry and sexual misconduct of the pagans, who have rejected the truth of God (*1:18-32*), and to God's wrath. But the Jews, in Paul's view, behaved no better, despite having the law. This aspect is developed in 2:1-3:9. In 2:9 Paul says: 'There will be anguish and distress for everyone who does evil, the Jew first and also the Greek.' Paul explains that, despite their possession of the law, the Jews are no better off, for all are under the power of sin.

The strong emphasis on sin in the first three chapters of Romans serves to underline the utterly gratuitous gift of justification brought by Jesus Christ, a gift available for all human beings.

What Kind of Text?

In the first part of our text the theme of the righteousness of God is examined. God's righteousness is revealed in the gospel of Jesus Christ, and is accepted by faith (*3:21-31*). In 4:1-5 Paul begins to look at the example of Abraham, who was justified by faith and not by his deeds. Paul in fact continues to examine Abraham's faith until 4:25.

Within our chosen passage there is a good example of a rhetorical diatribe, a kind of imaginary debate, in 3:27-31. Rhetorical questions abound.

The Sacrifice of Abraham by Laurent De La Hire.

Commentary: verse by verse reading

How God's Righteousness Works

Galatians 3:23-26 describes the temporary role of the law in this way:

Now before faith came, we were imprisoned and guarded under the law until faith would be revealed. Therefore the law was our disciplinarian (Greek paidagogos) until Christ came, so that we might be justified by faith. But now that faith has come, we are no longer subject to a disciplinarian, for in Christ Jesus you are all children of God through faith.

v.21 'But now!' says Paul. This is the 'now' of the final age brought about by God. Paul is speaking of a new time 'outside the law' (Greek *choris nomou*). This is a better rendering than 'irrespective of law' in the New Revised Standard Version translation. The righteousness of God, God's way of being just, is made known in this new time, the time of Jesus Christ. It has already been 'witnessed to' by the law and the prophets, in other words, in the Jewish Scriptures.

Paul has already referred to the gospel being promised in an earlier time in the opening words of the letter. God promised the gospel beforehand 'through his prophets in the holy scriptures' (*1:2*). Paul has shown, in particular, how the prophet Habakkuk foreshadows faith in Jesus Christ with his words 'the righteous one will live by faith' (*2:4*).

v.22 God's righteousness is bestowed 'through faith in Jesus Christ'. This is the very essence of Paul's gospel. We are saved by faith in Jesus. Since the literal wording of the Greek is 'the faith of Jesus Christ', some have interpreted this phrase as 'through the faithful witness of Jesus Christ'. This does not match Paul's basic message, with its emphasis on the Christian's faith in Jesus. God's gift is available to all who believe, because of their faith, without distinction, whether Jew or Gentile.

Romans 10:9-10 If you confess with your lips that Jesus is Lord and believe in your heart that God raised him from the dead, you will be saved. For one believes with the heart and so is justified, and one confesses with the mouth and so is saved.

v.23 Paul recalls what he explained at length earlier, that all, both Gentiles and Jews, have sinned. Both Jews and Gentiles have 'missed the mark', which is essentially what sin is. To sin is to fail to attain a moral standard, and to transgress against a law of God. It is to commit personal acts in thought and deed from which evil results. Paul adopts the teaching of the Old Testament, and in particular of Genesis, about the universality of the contagion brought about by sin. To 'fall short of the glory of God' may refer both to the 'glory' of living as God's children in this life and the prospect of glory in the life to come.

v.24 In the opening verses of the letter Paul had referred to receiving 'grace and apostleship' (*1:5*). He had wished the Roman community 'grace and peace' (*1:7*). Now he uses the word 'grace' (Greek *charis*) in connection with the justification which comes from faith. *Charis*, which recalls the covenant loving kindness of God, is now revealed in a new way through faith in Jesus Christ. Human beings are justified not by their own power or by their own good deeds but through the free gift of God.

In this context we encounter for the first time the word 'redemption' (Greek *apolutrosis*). In Romans 8:23 the word appears again, this time in relation to the end of time: 'We ourselves, who have the first fruits of the Spirit, groan inwardly while we wait for adoption, the redemption of our bodies.'

Human beings are not only justified, made righteous by God, but also 'redeemed'. The term 'redemption' takes us back to the idea of buying freedom, 'ransoming' or 'redeeming', an action attributed to God particularly in the second part of the book of Isaiah. God is described as the *go'el*, the 'redeemer' of Israel, who has freed them from the land of exile.

Isaiah 41:14 Your Redeemer is the Holy One of Israel.

Isaiah 44:24 Thus says the Lord, your Redeemer, who formed you in the womb.

In ancient Israelite society the *go'el* was the family member who had the duty of avenging the blood of a relative who had been murdered (as seen in *Numbers 35:19*). The *go'el* could also buy the freedom of a relative who had been enslaved, and provide protection for widows (as in *Ruth 2:20*). In the Letter to the Romans redemption means that Christ has liberated or ransomed enslaved human beings through his death on the cross.

Numbers 35:19 The avenger of blood must put the murderer to death. When he meets him he must put him to death.

Ruth 2:20 Naomi also said to Ruth: 'The man is a relative of ours, one of our nearest kin (Hebrew go'alim – plural of go'el).'

v.25 Another term with deep roots in the Jewish Scriptures is translated in NRSV as 'sacrifice of atonement'. The explanation is somewhat complex.

In the Book of Exodus Moses is told to construct a 'mercy seat' (Hebrew *kapporet*). The mercy seat is the cover or lid of the ark of the covenant, which was the shrine of God carried by the Israelites in their journeying, and the cherubim are the traditional guards of royal thrones. Exodus 25:17-18 reads: 'Then you shall make a mercy seat of pure gold. You shall make two cherubim of gold; you shall make them of hammered work, at the two ends of the mercy seat.'

Hebrews 9:3-5 is the only other New Testament text which refers to the mercy seat:

Behind the second curtain was a tent called the Holy of Holies. In it stood the golden altar of incense and the ark of the covenant overlaid on all sides with gold, in which there were a golden urn holding the manna, and Aaron's rod that budded, and the tablets of the covenant; above it were the cherubim of glory overshadowing the mercy seat.

In the New Revised Standard Version God makes Jesus 'a sacrifice of atonement', but a footnote gives the rendering 'a place of atonement'. The original meaning of the Hebrew term *kapporet*, which is translated as the Greek word *hilasterion* in Romans, is, as we have seen in the Exodus text, the 'mercy seat'. Paul states that God has made Jesus himself the 'mercy seat', and thereby made him the means for the forgiveness of sin. The Revised English Bible translates the term as 'the means of expiating sin' in an attempt to make this very difficult text of Paul clear.

Leviticus chapter 16 may provide some help. It tells of the ceremonies for the Day of Atonement, the most sacred day in the Jewish Year, known in Hebrew as *Yom Kippur*. Once a year, on this feast, the high-priest incenses the mercy seat and sprinkles animal blood upon it. The other priests are only allowed to sprinkle the blood of sin offerings on the veil of the sanctuary (*Leviticus 4:6 and 17*). By calling Christ the 'mercy seat', Paul shows that it is not through the sacrifices of the law that forgiveness is won, but through Christ's blood, through his death and resurrection.

v.26 The forbearance of God is demonstrated not only in relation to past sins but also to present ones. In verses 25-26 Paul twice stresses that this shows God's righteousness, his way of being just.

Jews Praying in the Synagogue on Yom Kippur by Maurycy Gottlieb.

No Room for Boasting

v.27 Paul strongly asserts that any boasting and self-congratulation must be excluded, because salvation is not achieved by human works, but by faith in Christ. Reliance on self should be replaced by reliance on God. For Paul the 'law of faith' replaces the 'law of works'.

v.28 Once again the principle is repeated that justification is by faith and not by the works of the law.

In his translation of the Letter to the Romans Martin Luther wrote 'only by faith'. Earlier writers had in fact written of salvation 'by faith alone' (Latin *sola fide*). This clearly adds to the Greek original. The Council of Trent, which, in 1547, responded to the reformation controversies, stated in its Decree on Justification that to affirm that human beings are justified by faith alone does not rule out human cooperation in the grace of justification.

The Letter to the Ephesians relates justification by faith to salvation, and to good works: 'For by grace you have been saved through faith, and this is not your own doing; it is the gift of God – not the result of works, so that no one may boast. For we are what he has made us, created in Christ Jesus for good works, which God prepared beforehand to be our way of life' (*2:8-10*).

vv.29-30 Paul again asserts that justification by faith in Christ is open both to Jew and Gentile. He uses the terms 'circumcision' and 'uncircumcision' to refer to Jews and Gentiles, terms translated in the NRSV as 'the circumcised' and 'the uncircumcised'. Paul speaks similarly in Galatians 2:8 of Jews as 'the circumcision'.

v.31 We might ask how Paul can now say that he is 'upholding' the law. The true purpose of the law is to bring people to God. This can now be done through faith in Christ in a way that was never possible simply by obeying the law. What the law intended is now achieved through Christ. Later, in Romans 13:10, Paul affirms that 'love is the fulfilment of the law'.

The Council of Trent teaches:

When God touches man's heart through the illumination of the Holy Spirit, man himself is not inactive while receiving that inspiration, since he could reject it; and yet, without God's grace, he cannot by his own free will move himself toward justice in God's sight. (DS 1525)

Romans 10:12 reads: For there is no distinction between Jew and Greek; the same Lord is Lord of all and is generous to all who call on him. For 'everyone who calls on the name of the Lord shall be saved.'

The Example of Abraham

4:1 Paul now sets out to use the faith of Abraham, 'our ancestor according to the flesh', to prove his point, that the good works of the law are not what leads to justification.

v.2 Paul takes up again, from 3:27, the theme of boasting. Even Abraham, who was considered upright by God, has no reason to boast. Both the book of Genesis and Jewish writings contemporary to Paul stress the righteousness of Abraham. The Book of Sirach attributes his greatness to 'keeping the law of the Most High' (*Sirach 44:19*), but Genesis 15:6 has God declare him righteous before the law was given, and even before he was circumcised. This point is used by Paul to underline that Abraham cannot have been justified because he obeyed the law. It was his faith in God which led to his justification. This point will be fully explained in 4:10-11.

v.3 Paul quotes the crucial verse of Genesis 15:6: 'Abraham believed God, and it was reckoned to him as righteousness.' The Hebrew concept of 'believing' involves a commitment to and reliance on God, which is clearly evident from the moment when Abraham obeys the command of God to leave his home and travel to a new land (*Genesis 12*).

The idea of his faith 'being reckoned' or 'being credited' as righteousness has been interpreted in different ways. While Catholic tradition has considered this to be a real change in the status of the believer before God, some Reformation theologians looked upon it simply as a legal fiction, a justice that was 'imputed' and not genuine. This became part of the problem of the interpretation of 'justification by faith'.

Romans 4:10-11

How then was righteousness reckoned to Abraham? Was it before or after he had been circumcised? It was not after, but before he was circumcised. He received the sign of circumcision as a seal of the righteousness that he had by faith while he was still uncircumcised.

The Joint Declaration of the World Lutheran Federation and the Catholic Church (1999) provides the following clarification: 'By justification we are both declared and made righteous. Justification, therefore, is not a legal fiction. God, in justifying, effects what he promises; he forgives sin and makes us truly righteous.' (Appendix)

The Letter to the Galatians 3:6-9 elaborates further on the faith of Abraham: 'Just as Abraham 'believed God, and it was reckoned to him as righteousness,' so, you see, those who believe are the descendants of Abraham. And the scripture, foreseeing that God would justify the Gentiles by faith, declared the gospel beforehand to Abraham, saying, 'All the Gentiles shall be blessed in you.' For this reason, those who believe are blessed with Abraham who believed.'

vv.4-5 Paul explains again that the righteousness bestowed on the sinner by God is a free gift, and not something that can be earned. Paul had written in Galatians 2:16: 'We know that a person is justified not by the works of the law but through faith in Jesus Christ. And we have come to believe in Christ Jesus, so that we might be justified by faith in Christ, and not by doing the works of the law, because no one will be justified by the works of the law.'

How are we to reconcile 'justification by faith alone' and 'justification by faith lived out in good works', the idea presented in the Letter of James? There is in fact no contradiction. It is God who justifies and saves us and this is a gift we can never deserve. Human willingness to receive this gift is shown by faith. Faith, however, cannot be reduced to an intellectual assent to God. It must, as James says, be lived out by actions. See James 2:21-26.

Christ the Redeemer at the peak of Corcovado mountain Rio de Janeiro, Brazil.

The Word Lives On

The Letter to the Romans is read in weeks 28 to 31 of the ferial lectionary, in Year 1. Romans 3:21-30 is read on the Thursday of the 28th week and Romans 4:1-8 on the Friday.

Romans 3:21-25,28 is also read in Year A on the Ninth Sunday in Ordinary Time.

Live the Word of God

Listen once more to the reading.

Suggestions for reflection and prayer

Paul is totally convinced that the loving kindness of God brings people to salvation as long as they have faith in Christ.

❖ Do I accept Paul's gospel, that I am saved by the love of God and not by my own good works?

Paul says that boasting is excluded.

❖ Am I inclined to pride in my faith and my achievements?

Paul cherishes the Scriptures and uses them to help people understand the coming of Christ.

❖ How deeply do I value the Jewish Scriptures?

'Faith works through love.' (Galatians 5:6)

❖ How loving is my faith?

St Therese of Lisieux wrote in the 'Story of a Soul':

After earth's exile, Lord, I hope to go and enjoy you in the fatherland, but I do not want to lay up merits for heaven. I want to work for your love alone. In the evening of this life, I shall appear before you with empty hands, for I do not ask you, Lord, to count my works. All our justice is blemished in your eyes. I wish, then, to be clothed in your own justice and to receive from your love the eternal possession of yourself. (Catechism of the Catholic Church 2011)

St Thérèse of Lisieux.

Adam and Christ

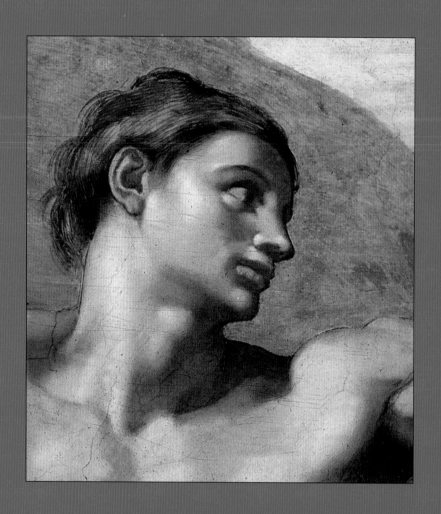

Hear the Word of God

Romans 5:1-21

[1] Therefore, since we are justified by faith, we have peace with God through our Lord Jesus Christ, [2] through whom we have obtained access to this grace in which we stand; and we boast in our hope of sharing the glory of God. [3] And not only that, but we also boast in our sufferings, knowing that suffering produces endurance, [4] and endurance produces character, and character produces hope, [5] and hope does not disappoint us, because God's love has been poured into our hearts through the Holy Spirit that has been given to us.

[6] For while we were still weak, at the right time Christ died for the ungodly. [7] Indeed, rarely will anyone die for a righteous person—though perhaps for a good person someone might actually dare to die. [8] But God proves his love for us in that while we still were sinners Christ died for us. [9] Much more surely then, now that we have been justified by his blood, will we be saved through him from the wrath of God. [10] For if while we were enemies, we were reconciled to God through the death of his Son, much more surely, having been reconciled, will we be saved by his life. [11] But more than that, we even boast in God through our Lord Jesus Christ, through whom we have now received reconciliation.

[12] Therefore, just as sin came into the world through one man, and death came through sin, and so death spread to all because all have sinned — [13] sin was indeed in the world before the law, but sin is not reckoned when there is no law. [14] Yet death exercised dominion from Adam to Moses, even over those whose sins were not like the transgression of Adam, who is a type of the one who was to come.

[15] But the free gift is not like the trespass. For if the many died through the one man's trespass, much more surely have the grace of God and the free gift in the grace of the one man, Jesus Christ, abounded for the many. [16] And the free gift is not like the effect of the one man's sin. For the judgement following one trespass brought condemnation, but the free gift following many trespasses brings justification. [17] If, because of the one man's trespass, death exercised dominion through that one, much more surely will those who receive the abundance of grace and the free gift of righteousness exercise dominion in life through the one man, Jesus Christ.

[18] Therefore just as one man's trespass led to condemnation for all, so one man's act of righteousness leads to justification and life for all. [19] For just as by the one man's disobedience the many were made sinners, so by the one man's obedience the many will be made righteous. [20] But law came in, with the result that the trespass multiplied; but where sin increased, grace abounded all the more, [21] so that, just as sin exercised dominion in death, so grace might also exercise dominion through justification leading to eternal life through Jesus Christ our Lord.

Opposite: Creation of Adam (detail from the Sistine Chapel) by Michelangelo.

Understand the Word of God

This session will explore:

- ❖ the consequences of justification
- ❖ a comparison of Adam and Christ
- ❖ the meaning of 'original sin'

Setting in the Letter

In the previous chapters of the Letter to the Romans, and particularly in 3:21-31, Paul has explained how justification happens, how we pass from a state of sin to the life of grace. He has made clear that this is fundamentally through the action of God, through our Lord Jesus Christ, 'who was handed over to death for our trespasses and was raised for our justification' (*4:25*). Every Christian is called to welcome this gift of grace from God in faith. This is the starting point of chapter 5, which begins the second doctrinal section of the letter (*Romans 5-8*).

What Kind of Text?

The first doctrinal part of the letter covered the first four chapters and explored how Christians are justified by faith in Jesus Christ. In chapters 5 to 8 Paul will consider the consequences of this 'justification' for the life of the Christian. He has already described in graphic terms, in chapters 1 and 2, the plight of humanity without the gospel. Now we are to learn what a difference faith in Jesus makes.

In 5:1-11 Paul makes connections between the justifying action of God and the life of the Christian. Christians are now at peace with God. The emphasis in these verses is on the love of God, poured out by the Holy Spirit.

In verses 12-21 Paul puts before us a comparison of the first Adam and Christ, the second Adam. Sin and death came through Adam. Eternal life comes through Christ.

Art depicting Adam and Eve expelled from Garden of Eden.

Commentary: verse by verse reading

The Consequences of Justification

v.1 What are the consequences of God's free gift of justification? What does Christ bring to the believer? The first consequence, in Paul's view, is peace. 'We have peace with God, through our Lord Jesus Christ.' Peace is the Hebrew concept of *shalom*, of everything being as it should be.

Paul stresses throughout this chapter that whatever the Christian receives as a result of justification comes 'through our Lord Jesus Christ'. The same phrase will be found in verse 11, at the end of this first section, and in verse 21, at the end of this chapter. The same phrase will recur at the end of chapters 6, 7 and 8.

v.2 We also have 'access in faith to this grace in which we now stand'. The grace is the fact of being justified. The Greek word for 'access', *prosagoge*, is to be found again in the Letter to the Ephesians 2:18 to describe the admittance that both Jew and Gentile have found due to the saving work of Christ: 'For through Christ both of us have access in one Spirit to the Father'. In Ephesians 3:12 we read: 'In him (Christ Jesus our Lord) we have access to God in boldness and confidence through faith in him.'

'We boast of our hope for the glory of God.' Boasting in our own achievements was ruled out in 3:27-31. Boasting in the gift of God is however allowed. The future hope of Christians is to be drawn into the glory of God, into the very life of God.

vv.3-4 The Christian can also boast about afflictions endured. Sufferings can be seen as a grace, for they lead to endurance, the building of character, and hope. The Letter of James 1:3-4 also speaks of endurance (Greek *hupomone*): 'You know that the testing of your faith produces endurance; and let endurance have its full effect, so that you may be mature and complete, lacking in nothing.'

v.5 Hope (Greek *elpis*) is founded on the love of God. This is the love God has for us, mentioned again in verse 8. Paul speaks here of the role of the Holy Spirit for the first time in the letter. He will elaborate later on the presence in the Christian of the 'Spirit of him who raised Jesus from the dead' (*8:11*).

v.6 The greatest demonstration of the love of God for us is the death of Christ, of which Paul now speaks. While we were weak, or helpless, and unable to help ourselves, Christ died for us. Paul says that he died 'at the right time', the *kairos* planned by God, and 'for the ungodly', those who have no reverence for God.

vv.7-8 Paul digresses and speaks about the depth of love involved in dying for a righteous person. Much greater love is shown by Christ, who died for us while we were still sinners. This verse connects the death of Christ, which has been the theme of verses 6-8, with the love of God spoken of in verse 5.

vv.9-10 Justification was a gift given to sinners. Now that we are 'justified' we can be sure we will be 'saved' from the 'wrath of God' by the life of Jesus. These verses gather together several ways of speaking of God's saving gift. 'Salvation' here seems to suggest the definitive gift of God's life at the end of time. The 'wrath of God' was described by Paul in 1:18 as the consequence of human ungodliness and wickedness. 'Reconciliation' is the restoration of friendship with God and the achievement of peace which is the consequence of justification.

v.11 Given the richness of God's love demonstrated in justification, reconciliation and salvation, we can 'boast in God'. In verse 2, Paul allowed us to boast in 'our hope of sharing the glory of God'. In verse 3 we were invited to boast in 'our sufferings'. In this curious phrase, we 'boast in God through our Lord Jesus Christ'.

Paul speaks again of 'hope' in Romans:

Romans 8:24-25 For in hope we were saved. Now hope that is seen is not hope. For who hopes for what is seen? But if we hope for what we do not see, we wait for it with patience.

Romans 12:12 Rejoice in hope, be patient in suffering, persevere in prayer.

John 3:16 God so loved the world that he gave his only Son, so that everyone who believes in him may not perish but may have eternal life.

Christ and Adam

1 Corinthians 15:21-22 For since death came through a human being, the resurrection of the dead has also come through a human being; for as all die in Adam, so all will be made alive in Christ.

The Book of Wisdom (or the Wisdom of Solomon) was written in Greek in Egypt in the first century BC (or possibly even later). It found its way into the Greek Bible and thereby into the Christian Old Testament. Paul may not have been familiar with it, but the ideas found there were accessible to him from other sources and from contemporary teaching.

The Catechism of the Catholic Church, in paragraph 405, reads:

Although it is proper to each individual, original sin does not have the character of a personal fault in any of Adam's descendants. It is a deprivation of original holiness and justice, but human nature has not been totally corrupted: it is wounded in the natural powers proper to it, subject to ignorance, suffering and the dominion of death, and inclined to sin – an inclination to evil that is called 'concupiscence'.

v.12 The question might be raised, 'How can Christ's actions justify us?' Paul says: 'Consider Adam!' Just as the actions of Adam had consequences for all human beings, so it is also with the actions of Christ. What Paul does here is to compare what Christ brings to human beings with what Adam brought.

The consequences of the sin of Adam are the entry of sin into the world, and of death. The story in Genesis 3 makes clear that Adam and Eve brought sin into the world. The Book of Wisdom, written many centuries later, clearly suggests that death was another consequence of sin: 'Through the devil's envy death entered the world, and those who belong to his company experience it.' (*Wisdom 2:24*) According to Jewish thinking of Paul's day, Satan (the devil) had been cast out of paradise and was consequently envious of man's continuing presence there. Satan took the form of a serpent and brought about the expulsion of the man and the woman from paradise by tempting them to sin, as recounted in Genesis.

'Death spread to all because all have sinned.' Once again the book of Genesis helps our understanding. Genesis 6:11-12 speaks about the contagion of sin: 'Now the earth was corrupt in God's sight, and the earth was filled with violence. And God saw that the earth was corrupt; for all flesh had corrupted its ways upon the earth.'

There is much discussion about the meaning of the difficult phrase translated in the NRSV as 'because all have sinned'. The Latin Vulgate translation has 'in whom all have sinned', and thus implies that everyone sinned in Adam. The Greek of this phrase is most accurately translated as 'death spread to all, given that (Greek *eph' ho*) all have sinned'. The sin of Adam is not a personal fault of all human beings, but a deprivation of original holiness and justice, which has devastating consequences for the well-being of the human race.

vv.13-14 Paul does not yet follow up his remarks about the consequence of Adam's sin by speaking of Christ. Instead he digresses in these two verses and turns his attention to the period immediately after Adam, before the Law was given by Moses. As a consequence of sin death still 'exercised dominion'. Verse 14 says literally that 'death reigned'. The period before Moses and after Moses is similarly dominated by sin and death.

Paul then refers to Adam as a 'type' of the one to come, namely Christ. He means that Adam foreshadows Christ. But Christ, who is the 'antitype', vastly overshadows Adam in what he achieves.

Christ enters Hell to rescue Adam and Eve and all the Just, Italian School, (15th century).

v.15 Paul's real interest here is in what the work of Christ brings us, and how much greater it is than what results from the sin of Adam. In these verses he repeatedly argues: 'If this is true of Adam, how much more is achieved through Christ!'

This kind of argument is known in ancient rhetoric, the art of speech making, as an 'a minori ad maius' argument, which is Latin for 'from smaller to greater'. Paul has already used the same kind of argument in verses 9 and 10, and it will be found again in verse 17. It is introduced by the words 'much more surely'.

Paul uses the a minori ad maius *argument in another letter:*

2 Corinthians 3:9 *For if there was glory in the ministry of condemnation, much more does the ministry of justification abound in glory!*

Paul uses the Greek word *charisma*, which literally means a gift of grace, a 'free gift', to refer to what Christ achieves. He stresses that the actions of Christ are far more effective than the sin of Adam. When Paul speaks of the consequences of Christ's action 'for the many' he effectively means all, as becomes clear in verse 18.

v.16 He compares the 'gift' to the 'sin'. Adam's sin brings condemnation, while Christ's gift brings justification. Paul uses a new word for justification, *dikaioma*. The richness of the Greek language also allows him to use two different words for 'free gift' in this verse, first *dorema* and then *charisma*. The second Greek word stresses the gratuitousness of the gift and may be more appropriate for a gift from God.

v.17 Throughout these verses Paul is cleverly repeating, with different words and different emphases, the same basic point. What Christ has done is infinitely better than what Adam did! Paul the preacher and speech-maker is using his rhetorical skills to the full.

In this verse Paul returns to the language of 'reigning' (in the NRSV translation 'exercised dominion') which he had used in verse 14 concerning death. Death reigned because of Adam, but those who receive the free gift of justification themselves reign in life because of Christ.

v.18 Paul emphasises that the one act of Adam and the one act of Christ affect all. He also takes up the theme of life. Justification and life come to all through Christ. Paul uses yet another word here for 'justification', the Greek word *dikaiosis*.

v.19 Approaching the comparison in yet another way in this verse, Paul compares the obedience of Christ to the disobedience of Adam.

When the text says 'many were made sinners' the sense is of 'being established as sinners' through the entry of sin into the world brought about by Adam. This perhaps helps us to understand better the concept of 'original sin'. We are born into a situation of sin and distance from God.

When Paul says that 'many will be made righteous' he is referring to the idea of 'being established as righteous' or being justified and saved through faith in Jesus.

v.20 The coming of the law of Moses led to the multiplication of offences, but where sin multiplied, grace abounded even more. The word he uses here for 'abounded' contrasts sharply with the weaker word 'multiplied', which he uses of the spread of sin. While the 'gift in grace' had been abundant in verse 15, here the Greek word indicates that grace is superabundant. The Latin translation may help here. It has *abundavit* in verse 15 and *superabundavit* in verse 20.

v.21 For the final time Paul uses the word 'reign' (in the NRSV 'exercise dominion'). While sin has reigned in death, grace, which has 'abounded all the more', 'will reign through justification to eternal life'. It is the grace of God which has the ultimate victory. All of this is brought about 'through Jesus Christ our Lord'. Chapters 6, 7 and 8 will have similar conclusions to stress at every stage of the argument that the grace of justification comes from Jesus.

Paul speaks again of the obedience of Jesus in the hymn in the Letter to the Philippians 2:6-8:

Christ Jesus, though he was in the form of God, did not regard equality with God as something to be exploited, but emptied himself, taking the form of a slave, being born in human likeness. And being found in human form, he humbled himself and became obedient to the point of death – even death on a cross.

*O loving wisdom of our God!
When all was sin and shame,
A second Adam to the fight
And to the rescue came.*

*O wisest love! that flesh and blood,
Which did in Adam fail,
Should strive afresh against
the foe,
Should strive and should prevail.*

(Blessed John Henry Newman)

Blessed John Henry Newman.

The Word Lives On

This passage of Romans has had enormous significance in theological debate, and has been studied intensely in order to try to explain the consequences of the sin of Adam.

Romans 5:12-21 is not surprisingly placed at the start of Lent in the lectionary, for it sums up the consequences of Adam's sin and of the saving work of Jesus Christ. Romans 5:12-19 is read on the First Sunday of Lent in Year A, when the first reading is the story of the sin of Adam in Genesis 2 and 3.

A shortened version of Romans 5:1-11 is read in Year A on the Third Sunday of Lent. Verses 1-5, with their references to Christ and to the Holy Spirit, are proclaimed on Trinity Sunday in Year C. Verses 5-11, which speak of the love of God poured into our hearts through the Holy Spirit, are read on the Solemnity of the Sacred Heart in Year C. The prominence of this chapter on these major feasts shows how completely these verses are considered to speak of the loving action of God through Jesus Christ in the Holy Spirit.

In the ferial lectionary a shorter version of Romans 5:12-21 is read on the Tuesday of the 29th week in Year 1.

Adam by Antonio Rizzo.

Live the Word of God

Listen once more to the reading.

Suggestions for reflection and prayer

Paul is insistent that the grace of God in Christ overrides all the influence of sin.

- ❖ Do I accept Paul's gospel?

- ❖ Has he convinced me?

- ❖ Or am I just confused by the idea of justification?

- ❖ How do I understand the story of Adam and Eve in the book of Genesis?

- ❖ Do I have a proper grasp of what original sin is?

See the quotation from the Catechism of the Catholic Church (paragraph 405) earlier in the commentary.

- ❖ How do I allow the life of the justified to thrive in me?

- ❖ Do I appreciate that the love of God has been poured into my heart through the gift of the Holy Spirit?

St John Chrysostom explains:

The free gift is much greater than the judgement. For it was not just Adam's sin which was done away with by the free gift but all other sins as well. And it was not just that sin was done away with – justification was given too. So Christ did not merely do the same amount of good that Adam did of harm, but far more and greater good. (Homilies on Romans 10)

Adam and Eve.

Baptism into Christ

Hear the Word of God

Romans 6:1-14

[1] What then are we to say? Should we continue in sin in order that grace may abound? [2] By no means! How can we who died to sin go on living in it? [3] Do you not know that all of us who have been baptised into Christ Jesus were baptised into his death? [4] Therefore we have been buried with him by baptism into death, so that, just as Christ was raised from the dead by the glory of the Father, so we too might walk in newness of life.

[5] For if we have been united with him in a death like his, we will certainly be united with him in a resurrection like his. [6] We know that our old self was crucified with him so that the body of sin might be destroyed, and we might no longer be enslaved to sin. [7] For whoever has died is freed from sin. [8] But if we have died with Christ, we believe that we will also live with him. [9] We know that Christ, being raised from the dead, will never die again; death no longer has dominion over him. [10] The death he died, he died to sin, once for all; but the life he lives, he lives to God. [11] So you also must consider yourselves dead to sin and alive to God in Christ Jesus.

[12] Therefore, do not let sin exercise dominion in your mortal bodies, to make you obey their passions. [13] No longer present your members to sin as instruments of wickedness, but present yourselves to God as those who have been brought from death to life, and present your members to God as instruments of righteousness. [14] For sin will have no dominion over you, since you are not under law but under grace.

Opposite: Baptismal font in the ruins of the Church of St Mary, Ephesus, Turkey.

Understand the Word of God

This session will explore:

- ❖ being baptised into Christ Jesus
- ❖ the Christian attitude to sin
- ❖ the new life of grace

Setting in the Letter

We continue with the second doctrinal section of the letter, which goes from chapter 5 to chapter 8. In chapter 5, Paul spelt out the consequences of what Christ did. Christians live now in a new kind of life, having been justified and reconciled by a compassionate and forgiving God. This gift is received through faith and not through the works of the law.

In this new section Paul spells out in more depth the moral consequences of this new life. It is inconceivable that a person who has received God's grace through Christ should continue in sin.

What Kind of Text?

Chapter 6 begins with the question 'What then are we to say?' Paul is embarking on a new argument, as he will do again in the same way in 6:15 – 'What then?' - and 7:7 – 'What then are we to say?' In each case there follows a rhetorical question and the response 'By no means!'

Paul is using the rhetorical device known as *reductio ad absurdum*. He introduces a mistaken statement in order to reject it. Should we remain in sin? Of course not!

This section contains a detailed explanation of the significance of baptism, and of the Christian's dying and rising with Christ. There is a repeated emphasis on this intimate union with Christ.

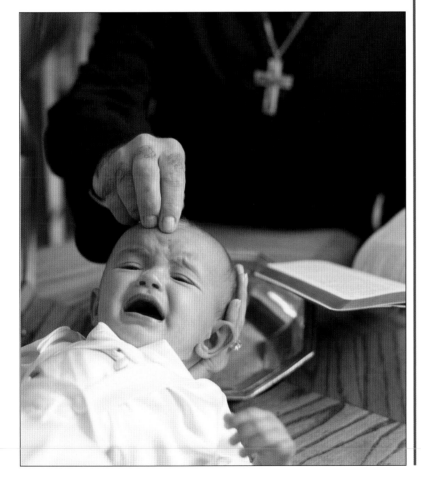

Baby boy at baptism.

Commentary: verse by verse reading

Dying with Christ

vv.1-2 The starting-point of Paul's argument is the question about sinning. Paul had referred earlier in the letter to the way some people had been deriving mistaken conclusions from his preaching by saying, 'Let us do evil so that good may come.' (*3:8*) In the final verses of chapter five Paul had explained that an abundance of sin led to an even greater abundance of grace. To go on sinning, it could be argued, would multiply grace in the world, which was surely a good thing.

Paul dismisses this idea as ludicrous. 'By no means' is our translation here. The phrase is literally 'Let it not be so!' We might translate it as 'Of course not!' or with the more colloquial phrase 'No way!'

Paul used the same phrase in Romans 3:31 'Do we then overthrow the law by this faith? By no means! On the contrary, we uphold the law.' A further use comes in Romans 7:7 'What then should we say? That the law is sin? By no means!' Paul is skilled in his use of these rhetorical techniques.

v.3 A further rhetorical flourish introduces the meat of the argument 'Do you not know?' Of course they do, for Paul is now speaking about the basics of Christian life. Baptism 'into Christ Jesus' is baptism into his death.

Elsewhere in the New Testament we read of baptism being given 'in the name' either of Jesus or of the Trinity. Peter encourages baptism 'in the name of Jesus Christ' in the speech at Pentecost in Acts 2:38. In the account of the appearance of the Risen Jesus in Matthew 28:19 we read the command to baptise 'in the name of the Father and of the Son and of the Holy Spirit'. This text points to a widespread practice in the early Church.

Here in Romans we read of being baptised 'into Christ Jesus'. Similarly Galatians 3:27 reads: 'All you who were baptised into Christ have clothed yourselves with Christ.' This expression speaks of the intimate association with Christ experienced by the believer. This is exactly

The Constitution on the Sacred Liturgy of Vatican II states:

But Christ also willed that the work of salvation, which the apostles preached, they should enact through the sacrifice and sacraments around which the entire liturgical life revolves. Thus by Baptism men and women are implanted in the paschal mystery of Christ; they die with him, are buried with him, and rise with him. (Sacrosanctum Concilium 6)

what Paul means here in Romans. Baptism into Christ is baptism into his death. It is a dying with Christ.

v.4 Paul makes things even clearer by saying 'we have been buried with him'. The Greek says literally 'we were co-buried with him' (Greek *sunetaphemen*). Paul loves to use such words to emphasise how Christians belong with Christ. In Colossians 2:12 he stresses once more how the Christian is drawn into the death and resurrection of Christ. He writes 'When you were buried (literally 'co-buried') with him in baptism, you were also raised (literally 'co-raised') with him through faith in the power of God, who raised him from the dead.'

Death leads to burial, and burial leads to resurrection. All these stages the Christian shares with Christ through baptism. Paul says that Jesus was raised 'by the glory of the Father'. In the Hebrew Scriptures it is the glory (Hebrew *kabod*) of the Lord which accomplishes marvels, and is witnessed by Moses and the people.

As so often through the New Testament it is stated that Jesus is raised by the power of the Father. Sharing in Christ's resurrection means that the Christian will now 'walk in the newness of life'. To walk of course refers to the whole moral behaviour of the Christian. In 2 Corinthians 5:17 Paul says: 'So if anyone is in Christ, there is a new creation: everything old has passed away; see, everything has become new!' Sin has no place in this new life.

v.5 In this verse Paul uses a fascinating image. When our translation says, 'we have been united with him', what the Greek suggests is that we 'have grown together (Greek *sumphutoi*) with him', like a shoot grafted on to a plant, both in his death and in his resurrection. The Christian is grafted on to the shoot which is Christ in order to receive his life, just as a grafted shoot receives sap from its host. This is an intimate, rich image which is lost in the translation.

The Decree on Ecumenism of Vatican II states:

By the sacrament of Baptism, whenever it is properly conferred in the way the Lord determined and is received with the proper dispositions of soul, people become truly incorporated into the crucified and glorified Christ and are reborn to a sharing of the divine life. (Unitatis Redintegratio 22)

Exodus 16:10 As Aaron spoke to the whole congregation of the Israelites, they looked toward the wilderness, and the glory of the Lord appeared in the cloud.

Exodus 24:17 Now the appearance of the glory of the Lord was like a devouring fire on the top of the mountain in the sight of the people of Israel.

Paul obviously finds the image of grafting very useful. In Romans 11:17-19 he will tell the Gentiles that they have been grafted on to the stock of the Jews: But if some of the branches were broken off, and you, a wild olive shoot, were grafted in their place to share the rich root of the olive tree, do not boast over the branches. If you do boast, remember that it is not you that support the root, but the root that supports you.

v.6 Paul speaks of our 'old self' (literally our 'old man') being crucified (literally 'co-crucified') with Christ. In Galatians 2:19-20 Paul wrote: 'I have been co-crucified with Christ; and it is no longer I who live, but it is Christ who lives in me.' The destruction of 'the body of sin', which means the human being closed to the Spirit and drawn to sin, what Paul later calls the 'body of death' (*7:24*), is the result. This is his answer to those who said 'let us go on sinning so that grace may be multiplied'. Slavery to sin must come to an end.

In the next chapter Paul admits that the struggle to choose the good continues: 'With my mind I am a slave to the law of God, but with my flesh I am a slave to the law of sin.' (*7:25*) In Romans 16:18 he draws a contrast between those who 'serve our Lord Jesus Christ' and those who serve 'their own appetites'.

v.7 'Whoever has died is freed from sin.' A literal translation would be: 'Whoever has died has been justified from sin.' The sentence is ambiguous, but seems to refer to death with Christ in baptism which brings forgiveness from sin.

New Life in Christ

v.8 Death with Christ leads to life with him. The emphasis here is on the life still in the future, the life of being with the Lord for ever, described in 1 Thessalonians 4:17, 'we will be with the Lord for ever'. Yet, this life is already experienced in the present life due to baptism. 2 Corinthians 5:17, quoted above in the commentary on verse 4, speaks about the 'new creation' which anyone who is in Christ already experiences.

v.9 Faith in our own resurrection comes from knowing that Christ was raised from the dead, and dies no more. Paul says that death no longer 'has dominion' over him, and uses a Greek word related to *kurios* (Greek for 'Lord'). Death no longer 'lords it' over Christ, for Christ has become Lord through his death and resurrection. As the hymn quoted by Paul in the Letter to the Philippians says, God's exaltation of Jesus means that all people should confess 'that Jesus Christ is Lord to the glory of God the Father' (*Philippians 2:11*).

v.10 Christ 'died to sin' and 'lives to God'. It must be the same with the Christian, who, having died to sin, is 'alive to God in Christ Jesus'.

In speaking of the death of Christ Paul uses the Greek expression *ephapax*, which means 'once and for all'. It is frequent in the Letter to the Hebrews. The writer of this letter presents Christ as the new high-priest, who offers himself as the one sacrifice for sin which brings to an end the sacrifices of the old covenant.

v.11 Through baptism into the death of Christ Christians must now consider themselves 'alive to God', because they are now 'in Christ Jesus'. Paul will use this phrase later in the letter. In 8:1, as he prepares to speak of the new life in the Spirit, we read 'There is no condemnation for those who are in Christ Jesus.' In 12:5 he states: 'We are one body in Christ.'

Hebrews 7:27 Unlike the other high priests, he has no need to offer sacrifices day after day, first for his own sins, and then for those of the people; this he did once and for all when he offered himself.

Hebrews 9:12 He entered once and for all into the Holy Place, not with the blood of goats and calves, but with his own blood, thus obtaining eternal redemption.

Hebrews 10:10 And it is by God's will that we have been sanctified through the offering of the body of Jesus Christ once and for all.

1 Corinthians 12:27 Now you are the body of Christ and individually members of it.

Ephesians 5:30 We are members of his body.

This verse brings to mind words from John's Prologue: The law indeed was given through Moses; grace and truth have come through Jesus Christ. (John 1:17)

v.12 The next three verses spell out in even more detail the practical consequences of having died and risen with Christ, of living 'in Christ'. Sin, which came into the world 'through one man' (*5:12*), must not be allowed to rule. We are no longer 'enslaved to sin' (verse 6). When Paul says 'do not let sin exercise dominion' he uses a word related to the Greek *basileus*, meaning 'king'. Sin should be neither 'lord' nor 'king' in the life of a Christian.

The Greek word for 'passions' or 'desires' *epithumiai* is found quite often in the writings of Paul. In Romans 13:14 he writes: 'Put on the Lord Jesus Christ, and make no provision for the flesh, to gratify its desires.'

Church teaching developed the idea of the 'passions' in human life and spoke of 'concupiscence' as the tendency to sin. Paul speaks of the struggle to avoid sin in the following chapter, especially in 7:14-20.

v.13 Paul encourages the Romans no longer to present their 'members' as 'instruments' or 'weapons' of wickedness. They should rather be 'instruments of righteousness'.

The Greek word for members is used for parts of the body in a similar sense in verse 19, and also in 7:5 and 7:23. The word is also used of individuals as 'members' of the body of Christ.

v.14 Paul concludes by repeating that sin is not to have dominion, not to be 'lord' over the Romans. 'You are not under the law but under grace.' This reference to the law prepares for the next section, and the next chapter in which Paul considers the difficult question of the law and sin, which has already surfaced earlier in the letter, particularly in Romans 2. It also prepares for the description of the life of grace, life in the Spirit, which comes in Romans 8.

Resurrection of Christ by Rembrandt.

The Word Lives On

It is not surprising that this text is read at Easter. Romans 6:3-11 is read at the Easter Vigil, shortly before the candidates for baptism are baptised. It is a powerful reminder of the significance of what they are about to undergo.

Romans 6:3-4 and 8-11 are also read on the Thirteenth Sunday in Ordinary Time in Year A, and on Wednesday of the twenty-ninth week of Ordinary Time Romans 6:12-18 is read.

Romans 6 may also be read at the celebration of baptism.

Paschal candle.

Live the Word of God

Listen once more to the reading.

Suggestions for reflection and prayer

Do I agree with those who say that we should continue in sin so that grace may abound?

❖ Do I allow sin to roam free in my life, relying on the loving mercy of God?

How seriously do I take my baptism?

❖ Am I aware that I have died with Christ to live a new life?

❖ Do I seek to renew my baptismal promises each Easter?

Am I eager to attract others to Christ and to his Church?

❖ Do I attempt to interest them in the gospel of Jesus Christ?

❖ Or do I prefer to hide my Christian identity?

What can I do to present myself more generously to God, and to make my members 'instruments of righteousness'?

From the Catechism of the Catholic Church:

Through Baptism the Christian is sacramentally assimilated to Jesus, who in his own baptism anticipates his death and resurrection. The Christian must enter into this mystery of humble self-abasement and repentance, go down into the water with Jesus in order to rise with him, be reborn of water and the Spirit so as to become the Father's beloved son in the Son, and 'walk in newness of life'. (537)

The Law of the Spirit of Life

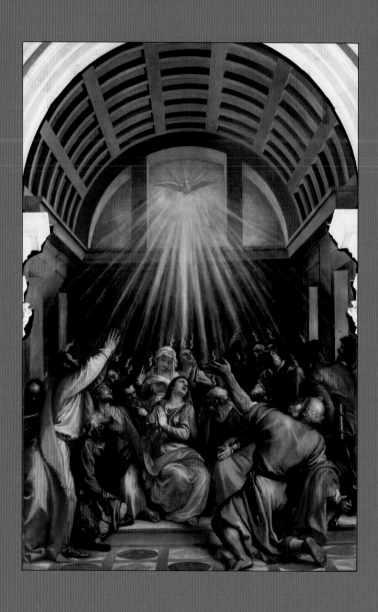

Hear the Word of God

Romans 8:1-17

[1] There is therefore now no condemnation for those who are in Christ Jesus. [2] For the law of the Spirit of life in Christ Jesus has set you free from the law of sin and of death. [3] For God has done what the law, weakened by the flesh, could not do: by sending his own Son in the likeness of sinful flesh, and to deal with sin, he condemned sin in the flesh, [4] so that the just requirement of the law might be fulfilled in us, who walk not according to the flesh but according to the Spirit. [5] For those who live according to the flesh set their minds on the things of the flesh, but those who live according to the Spirit set their minds on the things of the Spirit. [6] To set the mind on the flesh is death, but to set the mind on the Spirit is life and peace. [7] For this reason the mind that is set on the flesh is hostile to God; it does not submit to God's law—indeed it cannot, [8] and those who are in the flesh cannot please God.

[9] But you are not in the flesh; you are in the Spirit, since the Spirit of God dwells in you. Anyone who does not have the Spirit of Christ does not belong to him. [10] But if Christ is in you, though the body is dead because of sin, the Spirit is life because of righteousness. [11] If the Spirit of him who raised Jesus from the dead dwells in you, he who raised Christ from the dead will give life to your mortal bodies also through his Spirit that dwells in you.

[12] So then, brothers and sisters, we are debtors, not to the flesh, to live according to the flesh— [13] for if you live according to the flesh, you will die; but if by the Spirit you put to death the deeds of the body, you will live. [14] For all who are led by the Spirit of God are children of God. [15] For you did not receive a spirit of slavery to fall back into fear, but you have received a spirit of adoption. When we cry, 'Abba! Father!' [16] it is that very Spirit bearing witness with our spirit that we are children of God, [17] and if children, then heirs, heirs of God and joint heirs with Christ—if, in fact, we suffer with him so that we may also be glorified with him.

Opposite: Pentecost by Titian.

Understand the Word of God

This session will explore:

❖ the new life of the Spirit

❖ the prophetic roots of the idea

❖ what it means to be children of God

Setting in the Letter

The second doctrinal section of the letter goes from chapter 5 to chapter 8. In chapter 5 Paul described how Christians are justified and reconciled by a God who is compassionate and forgiving. The love of God is poured into our lives by the Holy Spirit. Paul also compared the consequences of the actions of Adam with what Christ brings. While sin and death came into the world through Adam, eternal life comes through Christ.

In chapter 6 Paul explored the new life which comes through baptism. Christians die with Christ in order to rise again with him. They are therefore dead to sin and alive for God (6:11).

In chapter 7 Paul speaks of the ongoing struggle of life and highlights the role of the law and sin. Scholars question whether Paul is speaking of his own struggle or in general terms about the human situation. In the final verses he exclaims: 'Wretched man that I am! Who will rescue me from this body of death? Thanks be to God through Jesus Christ our Lord!' (7:24-25)

What Kind of Text?

Chapter 8 is arguably the most important chapter in the Letter to the Romans, and explores the role of the Holy Spirit. While verses 1-17, which we are now examining, describe life according to the Spirit, verses 18-30, our next session, will take up the theme of future glory.

Up to this point in Romans Paul had only occasionally mentioned the Holy Spirit, but these verses are dominated by reference to the Spirit, firstly in a repeated comparison to life 'according to the flesh', and then, in verses 14-17, in reference to what it means to be 'children of God'.

Romans 5:5 God's love has been poured into our hearts through the Holy Spirit that has been given to us.

Romans 7:6 We are slaves not under the old written code but in the new life of the Spirit.

Commentary: verse by verse reading

Living by the Spirit

v.1 The chapter opens on a very positive note. Now that Jesus Christ has come, the situation for humanity is completely different. Paul's 'now' echoes the same word in 3:21, where Paul had written, 'But now, outside the law, the righteousness of God has been disclosed.' We are in an entirely new age!

Condemnation was what Adam brought, as Paul explained when comparing Adam to Christ in 5:16: 'For the judgement following one trespass brought condemnation, but the free gift following many trespasses brings justification.' Those who were 'baptised into Christ Jesus' (*6:3*) now live 'in Christ Jesus'.

v.2 Paul now introduces the extraordinary phrase 'the law of the Spirit of life', creating a deliberate tension between 'law' and 'Spirit'. The 'law of sin and death' was what he had considered in the previous chapter. Now he juxtaposes the two 'laws'.

The Book of Consolation of the prophet Jeremiah is found in Jeremiah 30-31. In these chapters we find promises of restoration after the Babylonian exile. Similarly, Ezekiel, who was himself deported to Babylon, reassures the people of Judah, who have lost everything, that God has not abandoned them. The oracles of salvation of Ezekiel are found in chapters 33-48 of his book, and include the famous vision of the dry bones in 37:1-14. In this section too the prophet states that God will give the exiles a life-giving Spirit (37:14).

This reference to the 'law of the Spirit' is Paul's creation, but he seems once again to be inspired by the Hebrew prophets. Jeremiah in his Book of Consolation speaks of a 'new covenant', saying 'I will put my law within them, and I will write it on their hearts.' (*Jeremiah 31:33*) The prophet of the exile, Ezekiel, expresses the hope in this way: 'A new heart I will give you, and a new spirit I will put within you; and I will remove from your body the heart of stone and give you a heart of flesh. I will put my spirit within you, and make you follow my statutes and be careful to observe my ordinances.' (*Ezekiel 36:26-27*) The phrase 'the law of the Spirit' seems to be the result of Paul's reflection on these texts.

Paul states that this new law 'has set you free'. This recalls his statement in chapter 6 that those who have received baptism have been 'freed from sin and enslaved to God' (6:22). Some have questioned whether the word 'you' is correct. Would not Paul rather have written 'has set me free', given the struggle he speaks of in chapter 7? Others suggest that the text should read 'has set us free'. These 'corrections' have found their way into some of the ancient manuscript copies of the Letter to the Romans.

The fourth century parchment copies of the New Testament known as the Codex Sinaiticus and the Codex Vaticanus both have the reading 'has set you free', but the fifth century Codex Alexandrinus reads 'has set me free'. We can understand how a scribe who knew both versions might 'correct' the text and write 'has set us free'.

v.3 God in Christ has achieved what the law could not do owing to the weakness of the flesh. The law gave knowledge of sin, but could not overcome sin. Through taking on our flesh in the incarnation Christ 'has condemned sin in the flesh' so that, as verse 1 explained, there is now 'no condemnation' for us.

v.4 What the law required can be fulfilled because we walk now according to the Spirit, thanks to the saving work of God in Christ. The purpose of the law has been achieved.

v.5 Paul now spells out what it means to live 'according to the flesh' and 'according to the Spirit'. Human beings either 'set their mind' (Greek *phronein*) on things of the flesh or on things of the Spirit. Those who set their mind on things of the flesh exclude God and exclude others, thus setting aside the commandments of God.

Paul uses the same Greek verb phronein in the Letter to the Philippians:
Philippians 2:5 Let the same mind be in you that was in Christ Jesus.
Philippians 3:19 Their minds are set on earthly things.

v.6 Paul speaks of the goal or aspiration of those who live according to the flesh and those who live according to the Spirit, using the related Greek word *phronema*. The goal of the former is death, that of the latter 'life and peace'. Paul will later greet the Roman Christians with the words: 'The God of peace be with all of you.' (*15:33*)

vv.7-8 Paul then describes in more detail the attitude of those who live according to the flesh. It is an attitude of hostility to God. The Letter of James expresses a similar idea when it reads: 'Do you not know that friendship with the world is enmity with God?' (*James 4:4*) Such opposition to God means that the person does not submit to the law of God. In fact, says Paul, he cannot submit to it, and consequently cannot please God.

Saint Irenaeus comments:
The apostle does not reject the substance of flesh but shows that the Spirit must be infused into it. (Against Heresies 5.10.2)

The Spirit is in You

v.9 'But you!' Paul now addresses the Roman Christians directly. They are not 'in the flesh' because the Spirit of God dwells in them. He will now describe what life in the Spirit entails. He had already written to the Corinthians that they were 'temples of God' because the Spirit of God dwelt in them (*1 Corinthians 3:16*), and encouraged them to sexual morality because their bodies were 'temples of the Holy Spirit' (*1 Corinthians 6:19*).

v.10 'If Christ is in you,' says Paul, implying that the presence of the Spirit is inseparable from the presence of Christ. The body may be dead, but the spirit is life. Here he refers to the components of the person, the mortal body and the immortal spirit. Their human spirits are alive 'because of righteousness (Greek *dikaiosune*)'. He recalls God's righteousness and the saving work of Christ, which we describe as 'justification'.

v.11 But God does not disregard the mortal bodies of human beings. They will be raised up by the One who raised Christ from death. This is the work of the same Spirit 'that dwells in you'. Paul may be recalling Ezekiel's vision of the dry bones raised to life. Ezekiel had recorded these words of God: 'I will put my spirit within you, and you shall live.' (*Ezekiel 37:14*)

Galatians 5:19-21: Now the works of the flesh are obvious: fornication, impurity, licentiousness, idolatry, sorcery, enmities, strife, jealousy, anger, quarrels, dissensions, factions, envy, drunkenness, carousing and things like these. I am warning you, as I warned you before: those who do such things will not inherit the kingdom of God.

vv.12-13 These verses are something of a summary of the preceding argument. Christians owe no obligations to the flesh, for living according to the flesh leads to death. Paul does not complete the argument, but the implication is clear: Christians owe everything to Christ and to his Spirit. Paul lists 'the deeds of the body' which Christians must 'put to death' in Galatians 5:19-21, where he calls them 'the works of the flesh'. The final emphasis in this section is on life: if you do this, 'you will live'.

Children of God

v.14 The expression 'led by the Spirit' is found also in Galatians 5:18: 'If you are led by the Spirit, you are not subject to the law.' To be led by the Spirit is to be a 'son' of God. Note that the NRSV has 'children' due to its policy of 'inclusive language'.

The concept of divine sonship has its roots in texts from the Hebrew Bible. In the Book of Exodus, God refers to Israel as a firstborn son. If Pharaoh does not free him, his own firstborn will be punished (*Exodus 4:22-23*). In the opening verses of the Book of Isaiah these words of God are reported: 'I reared children and brought them up, but they have rebelled against me.' (*Isaiah 1:2*).

The presence of the Spirit identifies Christians as children of God. Galatians 4:6 has a similar explanation: 'Because you are sons, God has sent the Spirit of his Son into our hearts, crying, "Abba! Father!"'

Further references to Israel as son:

Jeremiah 31:9 'With weeping they shall come, and with consolations I will lead them back, I will let them walk by brooks of water, in a straight path in which they shall not stumble; for I have become a father to Israel, and Ephraim is my firstborn.'

Hosea 11:1 'When Israel was a child, I loved him, and out of Egypt I called my son.'

v.15 These children of God are not slaves, but truly sons and daughters. The spirit of slavery brings only fear, but the spirit of sonship leads the children of God to cry out in confidence to God. As in the passage from Galatians (*4:6*) it is the characteristic of the sons and daughters of God to cry out 'Abba!' Christians obviously treasured the use of this Aramaic word for 'Father', the word used by Jesus in the Passion Narrative of Mark (*14:36*), when he wrestles with the prospect of torture and death. Does Paul want the Romans to understand by this that God is available to assist those who have the Spirit of Christ even in times of pain and sorrow, persecution and martyrdom? This interpretation may be supported by the reference to suffering with Christ in verse 17.

v.16 When Paul asserts that the Spirit 'bears witness with' our spirit, he says literally that the Holy Spirit 'co-testifies' or 'co-witnesses' (Greek *summarturei*) with us. The Spirit empowers Christians to bear witness even in death, if they are willing to share the fate of the first martyr, Christ himself. Is Paul once again thinking of the persecution and danger faced by Christian witnesses?

Above: The Agony in the Garden by Giovanni Bellini.

The Spirit testifies that we are 'children of God' (Greek *tekna*). Earlier Paul had spoken of being 'sons'. Now his language echoes that of the Gospel of John.

v.17 The passage reaches a climax with 'if children, then heirs, heirs of God, co-heirs with Christ'. Paul rejoices that to be a child of God means that we shall inherit the gifts of the Father. In Galatians 4:7, in a similar context, he had written: 'You are no longer a slave but a son, and if a son then also an heir, through God.'

Once again, as we saw in Romans 6 (verse 4), Paul uses Greek verbs with the prefix *sun* meaning 'together with' to speak of experiences which Christians share with Christ. We are 'co-heirs' (Greek *sunkleronomoi)* of Christ, for we 'co-suffer' with him (Greek *sumpaschomen*) in order to be 'co-glorified' (Greek *sundoxasthomen*). In Romans 5:2-3 Paul had already written: 'We boast in our hope of sharing the glory of God. And not only that, but we also boast in our sufferings.' The Spirit empowers the Christian to follow the way of Christ from death to new life. Paul will speak further of the glory the Christian shares with Christ in the following verses.

John 1:12 To all who received him, who believed in his name, he gave power to become children of God.

John 11:51-52 Jesus was about to die for the nation, and not for the nation only, but to gather into one the dispersed children of God.

1 John 3:1 See what love the Father has given us, that we should be called children of God; and that is what we are.

Pieta by Giovanni Bellini.

The Word Lives On

Romans 8:8-11, with its emphasis on the life-giving role of the Spirit, is read on the Fifth Sunday of Lent in Year A. Romans 8:14-17, with its reference to Father, Son and Spirit, is read on Trinity Sunday in Year B.

In the ferial lectionary our text is part of the semi-continuous reading of the letter spread over four weeks. Romans 8:1-11 is heard on Saturday of Week 29 in Year 1, with Romans 8:12-17 read on the following Monday.

Holy Trinity by Andrei Rublev.

Live the Word of God

Listen once more to the reading.

Suggestions for reflection and prayer

Do I experience the freedom which the Spirit of life in Christ Jesus brings?

❖ In what ways do I impede the work of the Spirit in my life?

❖ What is my attitude to my flesh, my body?

❖ Do I allow the Spirit to bring life to my whole self and to guide my understanding and my actions?

❖ What kind of slavery still has a place in my life?

❖ What can I do to shake off the bonds which still entrap me?

❖ Can I at least begin to see how suffering with Christ might be a gift, rather than something to be avoided at all costs?

❖ How determined am I to persevere in living as a child of God, so that I may one day come to experience God's glory?

St Peter Chrysologus, bishop of Ravenna from 433 until 450, writes:

Our awareness of our status as slaves would make us sink into the ground and our earthly condition would dissolve into dust, if the authority of our Father himself and the Spirit of his Son had not impelled us to this cry: 'Abba, Father!' When would a mortal dare call God 'Father', if his innermost being were not animated by power from on high? (Sermo 71,3)

The Glory to Come

Hear the Word of God

Romans 8:18-30

[18] I consider that the sufferings of this present time are not worth comparing with the glory about to be revealed to us. [19] For the creation waits with eager longing for the revealing of the children of God; [20] for the creation was subjected to futility, not of its own will but by the will of the one who subjected it, in hope [21] that the creation itself will be set free from its bondage to decay and will obtain the freedom of the glory of the children of God. [22] We know that the whole creation has been groaning in labour pains until now; [23] and not only the creation, but we ourselves, who have the first fruits of the Spirit, groan inwardly while we wait for adoption, the redemption of our bodies. [24] For in hope we were saved. Now hope that is seen is not hope. For who hopes for what is seen? [25] But if we hope for what we do not see, we wait for it with patience.

[26] Likewise the Spirit helps us in our weakness; for we do not know how to pray as we ought, but that very Spirit intercedes with sighs too deep for words. [27] And God, who searches the heart, knows what is the mind of the Spirit, because the Spirit intercedes for the saints according to the will of God.

[28] We know that all things work together for good for those who love God, who are called according to his purpose. [29] For those whom he foreknew he also predestined to be conformed to the image of his Son, in order that he might be the firstborn within a large family. [30] And those whom he predestined he also called; and those whom he called he also justified; and those whom he justified he also glorified.

Opposite: The Last Judgement by Fra Angelico.

Understand the Word of God

This session will explore:

- ❖ the groaning of creation
- ❖ being saved in hope
- ❖ the assistance of the Spirit
- ❖ God's plan for the good of all

Setting in the Letter

The second doctrinal section of the letter includes chapters 5 to 8. Chapter 8 is something of a climax. We have already examined verses 1-17 and their description of life according to the Spirit.

Verses 18-30 introduce the theme of 'glory'. Romans 3:23-24 had taught that 'all have sinned and fall short of the glory of God', but that 'they are now justified by his grace as a gift, through the redemption that is in Christ Jesus'. Paul's reflection will considerably develop this theme.

What Kind of Text?

Verses 18-30 begin with another reference to suffering, which follows naturally from verse 17. Paul now assures the Roman Christians that the coming glory will considerably outweigh whatever suffering they are called upon to endure. Paul then broadens the panorama by speaking of 'the whole creation' and its longing for freedom. Christians live in hope that the salvation announced to them will be realised. Paul also returns to the role of the Spirit, which 'intercedes for the saints' (verse 27).

Our text ends with a rhetorical climax which speaks of God's foreknowledge, and then of predestination, vocation, justification and glorification. The text begins and ends with the theme of glory.

The Garden of Eden with the Fall of Man by Bruegel and Rubens.

Commentary: verse by verse reading

Creation Set Free

v.18 The previous verse ended with reference to suffering with Christ in order to share his glory. Now Paul explains that the sufferings which have to be borne are as nothing compared with the glory to come. 'Glory' is a difficult concept to grasp. It invites us to look at the Hebrew concept of God's *kabod*, which, in speaking of the presence of God, also evokes the awe which that presence engenders. In Romans 5:2 Paul had written: 'We boast in our hope of sharing the glory of God.' To be drawn into the glory of God, to share that glory, is our hope, but it is for the present beyond our imagining. All this is what Christ offers to the Christian.

v.19 Paul introduces an astonishing new concept, the 'eager longing' of creation that the sons of God should be revealed. Paul says literally: 'the yearning of creation eagerly awaits the revelation of the sons of God'. The word he uses for 'yearning' (Greek *apokaradokia*) is only used once more by Paul when, in Philippians 1:20, he speaks of his yearning and hope that Christ be always exalted by his preaching. Creation experiences a yearning for the full and final revelation of what Christ's death and exaltation have brought about.

Paul speaks again, as in the previous verse, of things which are to be revealed. There is an apocalyptic, end-time tone to what he says. The glory of the revealing of the sons of God is not only longed for but somehow to be shared by all creation.

v.20 How is it that creation comes to share the desperate longing experienced by human beings? The answer seems to be given in this next extraordinary verse. 'The creation was subjected to futility by the one who subjected it in hope.' What is this 'futility' and who is the 'one' who subjected creation?

Scholars have debated these questions at great length. The clearest interpretation of this verse seems to be that it refers to the suffering of creation which came through the entry of sin and evil into the world. According to the narrative of Genesis chapter 3, the sin of the man and the woman brings pain and suffering, and the earth itself is cursed, when the Lord God says to the man: 'Cursed is the ground because of you.' (*Genesis 3:17*) The entry of pain and suffering into the creation is linked by Genesis to the spread of sin. Somehow, for reasons theologians have long grappled with, pain and suffering are shared by the whole creation.

When Paul speaks of the creation 'being subjected' he is possibly using a 'divine passive', which means 'God subjected it'. When he speaks of 'futility' (Greek *mataiotes*) it is helpful to recall the Hebrew concept of 'vanity' (Hebrew *hebel*), which can be translated 'uselessness', 'emptiness', 'futility'. The idea is found at the beginning of the book of Qoheleth (*Ecclesiastes*) with its repeated phrase 'vanity of vanities', and in 2 Kings 17:15 where the people 'go after false idols'. The Jerusalem Bible resorts to a paraphrase of Paul's statement and says 'creation was made unable to attain its purpose'. This might be going a little too far, for with God's intervention it will achieve its purpose.

However the pain of the world emerged, God is preparing glory, entry into the very life of God, for all God's creatures, through the saving work of Jesus Christ and in the power of the Spirit. Paul knows that the power and love of God are without limit.

Pope John Paul II wrote:

Above all, love is greater than sin, than weakness, than the 'futility of creation', it is stronger than death; it is a love always ready to raise up and forgive, always ready to go to meet the prodigal son, always looking for 'the revealing of the sons of God', who are called 'to the glory that is to be revealed'. This revelation of love is also described as mercy; and in man's history this revelation of love and mercy has taken a form and a name: that of Jesus Christ.

(*Redemptor Hominis 9*)

Expulsion from the Garden of Eden by Thomas Cole.

v.21 Paul spoke of the freedom brought by the new law of the Spirit in verse 2. In chapter 6 he taught that those who have received baptism have been 'freed from sin and enslaved to God' (6:22). Here it is the whole of creation which awaits liberation. What human beings receive from God through Jesus Christ, 'the freedom of the glory of the children of God', will be bestowed on creation too. The 'bondage to decay' once again recalls the Genesis story of the land cursed due to the sin of Adam.

v.22 Paul elaborates still further with a new image. If we examine the Greek text we see that Paul uses two verbs: the whole creation 'groans together' and 'suffers agony together' like a mother preparing to give birth. It is not simply God's human creation which yearns for freedom, but the whole of creation. Paul is adopting here an image used of the transition from winter to spring in Greek writers of the time, in which they spoke of the groaning earth giving birth to new life. Paul uses the same image of groaning in 2 Corinthians 5:2: 'For in this tent we groan, longing to be clothed with our heavenly dwelling.'

v.23 Despite the fact that Christians have already received the Spirit, they still groan in expectation. Christians at present have the 'first fruits' of the Spirit, for the fullness of the Spirit's gifts is still awaited. The term 'first fruits' (Greek *aparche*) is used primarily of the fruits of the harvest, but Paul uses the expression later in the letter about a convert called Epaenetus, whom he describes as 'the first fruits of Asia for Christ' (16:5).

The expectation of Christians is for the fullness of divine adoption, when they will be God's children completely. Redemption (Greek *apolutrosis*), as in 3:24, signifies the buying back into freedom of a slave. Christians are already free but the fullness of their freedom is yet to be realised. In speaking of the redemption of the body Paul stresses that the whole person will be saved.

vv.24-25 Paul spoke of hope when he mentioned in verse 20 that the creation was 'subjected to futility'. There is a universal tension towards the time when all creation will reach its God-given goal. We are 'saved in hope'. Despite the reality of salvation already experienced, Christians still live in hope of something as yet not seen. 'Patience' or 'endurance' (Greek *hupomone*) is therefore a necessity for the life of faith. Once again there is an implicit reference to suffering.

The Help of the Spirit

v.26 In a beautiful passage Paul stresses that the Spirit is on our side. The text is translated here as 'helps us in our weakness' but seems to speak of the Spirit standing in solidarity with us. This may suggest that the Spirit assists us in the general struggle of fidelity, but Paul focuses now on our inability to pray.

'We do not know how to pray as we ought' is more accurately translated 'we do not know what to pray'. Amid our own weakness the Spirit intercedes. Paul breaks new ground here, using expressions for which there is no biblical precedent. Those who intercede in the Jewish Scriptures are people or angels, and they do not emit 'sighs too deep for words'. The word for 'sigh' (Greek *stenagmos*) is of the same root as the verb used in verses 22-23 of the groaning of creation. Translators have understandably avoided referring to the 'groans of the Spirit'. These sighs or groans are *alaletoi*. They are 'not in speech', 'not in words'. Paul uses new language to evoke the inexpressible activity of the Spirit.

v.27 Paul does not use the word 'God' here but speaks of 'the One who searches hearts'. There are precedents to such language in the Old Testament, and the Book of Revelation uses identical words in 2:23 in the message of Christ to the church in Thyatira: 'All the churches will know that I am the one who searches minds and hearts.'

This God is aware of the aspiration or mind (Greek *phronema*) of the Spirit, who again is said to 'intercede', this time for 'the saints', God's holy people.

Called to Glory

v.28 When Paul speaks of 'all things' working together for good, he is surely including 'the sufferings of this present time' he mentioned in verse 18. Love of God is urged in the ancient forms of the decalogue (*Exodus 20:6* and *Deuteronomy 5:10*), and Paul seems here to use the phrase 'those who love God' to refer to all Christians.

There is some disagreement about the genuine text of Romans in this verse, with some trustworthy manuscripts having the reading 'God works all things for good'. The sense, however, would not be changed by this reading.

The 'purpose' of God is to be explained in the following verses. In Ephesians 1:11 we read that we are destined 'according to the purpose of him who accomplishes all things according to his counsel and will', and in Ephesians 3:11 we read of God's 'eternal purpose in Christ Jesus our Lord'. In his introduction to the letter Paul addressed the Roman Christians as 'called to belong to Jesus Christ' and 'called to be saints' (*1:6-7*).

v.29 Paul now goes through the stages of God's purpose in relation to human beings. God 'foreknows' them. This recalls the words of the Lord to the young Jeremiah at the moment of his call: 'Before I formed you in the womb I knew you' (*Jeremiah 1:5*). God 'predestined' them to be conformed to the image of Christ. This stage adds the element of a special purpose, election or vocation for each individual Christian. This is not of course the predestination of an individual to good or evil, but the desire of God that all people should be 'conformed to the image of his Son'. We read in 2 Corinthians 3:18: 'All of us, with unveiled faces, seeing the glory of the Lord as though reflected in a mirror, are being transformed into the same image from one degree of glory to another.' Thus Jesus is 'the firstborn among many brothers', a sense which is obscured by the translation in the NRSV 'the firstborn within a large family'.

Paul seems to have been familiar with Plato's 'Republic', written in the fourth century BC. In it we read:

Shall we not agree that all that comes from the gods turns out for the best for him who is dear to the gods?

Colossians 1:18 He is the beginning, the firstborn from the dead.

Revelation 1:5 Jesus Christ, the faithful witness, the firstborn of the dead.

v.30 The final stages of God's purpose are calling, justification and glorification. These stages are expressed in a grand rhetorical climax. Those who are called when they hear the Christian message are justified through faith in Christ, as Paul makes clear particularly in this letter. Justification leads to the life of glory, as he has been explaining in this chapter. This verse stresses the absolute sovereignty of God's plan.

The Word Lives On

In the ferial lectionary our text is part of the semi-continuous reading of the letter spread over four weeks. Romans 8:18-25 is heard on Tuesday of Week 30 in Year 1, with Romans 8:26-30 read on the Wednesday.

In the Sunday lectionary our passage is covered on Sundays 15 to 17 in Year A.

Not surprisingly 8:22-27, with the emphasis on the action of the Holy Spirit, is laid down to be read at the Vigil Mass of Pentecost.

The imagery of verse 21 on the freedom of creation is echoed in the Fourth Eucharistic Prayer: 'Then in your kingdom, freed from the corruption of sin and death, we shall sing your glory with every creature through Christ our Lord, through whom you give us everything that is good.'

From the Catechism of the Catholic Church:

The Holy Spirit, the artisan of God's works, is the master of prayer. (741)

Pope John Paul II.

Live the Word of God

Listen once more to the reading.

Suggestions for reflection and prayer

Do I understand that suffering, however unwelcome, has a place in God's plan for our glorification, even if we cannot fully grasp why?

Do I await with eager longing the revelation of the children of God?

❖ Do I experience and express this longing in prayer?

❖ How important is hope in my life?

❖ Do I realise that it is the future dimension of faith?

How often do I invoke the help of the Holy Spirit to assist me to pray?

❖ Do I trust that God's presence is mysterious and powerful if I open my heart and mind?

How broad is my vision of what awaits me?

❖ Do I yearn for the revelation of the children of God and the renewal of creation according to God's purpose?

Blessed John Paul II wrote in the Encyclical Redemptor Hominis in 1979:

Are we of the twentieth century not convinced of the overpoweringly eloquent words of the Apostle of the Gentiles concerning the 'creation that has been groaning in travail together until now' and 'waits with eager longing for the revelation of the sons of God', the creation that 'was subjected to futility'? Does not the previously unknown immense progress - which has taken place especially in the course of this century - in the field of man's dominion over the world itself reveal - to a previously unknown degree - that manifold subjection 'to futility'? It is enough to recall certain phenomena, such as the threat of pollution of the natural environment in areas of rapid industrialization, or the armed conflicts continually breaking out over and over again, or the prospectives of self-destruction through the use of atomic, hydrogen, neutron and similar weapons, or the lack of respect for the life of the unborn. The world of the new age, the world of space flights, the world of the previously unattained conquests of science and technology - is it not also the world 'groaning in travail' that 'waits with eager longing for the revealing of the sons of God'? (Redemptor Hominis 8)

The Absolute Freedom of God

Hear the Word of God

Romans 9:1-18

I am speaking the truth in Christ—I am not lying; my conscience confirms it by the Holy Spirit— 2 I have great sorrow and unceasing anguish in my heart. 3 For I could wish that I myself were accursed and cut off from Christ for the sake of my own people, my kindred according to the flesh. 4 They are Israelites, and to them belong the adoption, the glory, the covenants, the giving of the law, the worship, and the promises; 5 to them belong the patriarchs, and from them, according to the flesh, comes the Messiah, who is over all, God blessed for ever. Amen.

6 It is not as though the word of God had failed. For not all Israelites truly belong to Israel, 7 and not all of Abraham's children are his true descendants; but 'It is through Isaac that descendants shall be named after you.' 8 This means that it is not the children of the flesh who are the children of God, but the children of the promise are counted as descendants. 9 For this is what the promise said, 'About this time I will return and Sarah shall have a son.' 10 Nor is that all; something similar happened to Rebecca when she had conceived children by one husband, our ancestor Isaac. 11 Even before they had been born or had done anything good or bad (so that God's purpose of election might continue, 12 not by works but by his call) she was told, 'The elder shall serve the younger.' 13 As it is written, 'I have loved Jacob, but I have hated Esau.'

14 What then are we to say? Is there injustice on God's part? By no means! 15 For he says to Moses, 'I will have mercy on whom I have mercy, and I will have compassion on whom I have compassion.' 16 So it depends not on human will or exertion, but on God who shows mercy. 17 For the scripture says to Pharaoh, 'I have raised you up for the very purpose of showing my power in you, so that my name may be proclaimed in all the earth.' 18 So then he has mercy on whomsoever he chooses, and he hardens the heart of whomsoever he chooses.

Understand the Word of God

Setting in the Letter

We have reached a very significant part of the Letter to the Romans, but a part which is not very well known. Chapters 9 to 11 deal with the situation of the Jewish people after the coming of Christ. The chapters belong together as a kind of sermon on the topic, and there are those who suggest that Paul inserted here a sermon which he had written earlier. In fact, one could go from the end of chapter 8 to the beginning of chapter 12 and not miss these chapters.

Nevertheless, they deal with a crucial question, and one which was touched upon at the beginning of chapter 3, where Paul asked the question 'What advantage has the Jew? Or what is the value of circumcision?' He had answered his own question with 'Much, in every way!' Now he returns to the same question and asks what place the Jews now have in God's plan. He begins by expressing his deep regret that the majority of his Jewish brothers and sisters have not embraced faith in Christ.

What Kind of Text?

Chapter 9 begins with a deeply felt appeal (verses 1-5). The argument continues with frequent citations from the Scriptures. The same happened in chapter 4, when Paul examined the faith of Abraham, but generally in Romans direct biblical quotations are not frequent. Towards the end of the passage Paul enters into vigorous dialogue with his listeners: 'What then are we to say? Is there injustice on God's part? By no means!' This is the style of what the Greeks called 'diatribe', which included questions and answers and was used in philosophical works, with which Paul may have been familiar.

The Sabbath Meal.

Commentary: verse by verse reading

The Privilege of Israel

vv.1-2 Given that the Israelites had a special role in God's plan of revelation, how is it that they now seem to be marginalised? Paul expresses his deep sadness that they have not come to faith in Christ. Paul maintained from the outset of the letter that the good news was 'the power of God for salvation to everyone who has faith, to the Jew first and also to the Greek' (*1:16*). How is it that this power has been largely ineffective for the Jews? Paul's anguish must have been increased by the fact that, as apostle to the Gentiles, he might seem to have encouraged rejection of the gospel by the Jews.

Paul underlines the truth of what he writes. A similarly emphatic statement of the mission of Paul is backed up in 1 Timothy 2:7 by the same words, 'I am telling the truth, I am not lying.' Not content with this, Paul speaks of his conscience 'confirming' what he says 'in the Holy Spirit'. There is no doubt that Paul is speaking of something which is of the utmost importance to him, and deeply felt. He feels both sorrow and anguish.

v.3 From the depth of his feeling Paul expresses a wish that cannot be fulfilled, that he should be separated from Christ. He uses the Greek expression *anathema*, which is here translated by the phrase 'cursed and cut off'. The term reflects the ancient Hebrew idea of *herem,* which speaks of something to be placed under a ban of destruction for religious reasons. In the Book of Joshua (6:17), with its primitive sense of God, the city of Jericho is put under such a ban.

Paul uses the idea in several places. In the Letter to the Galatians, he delivers the curse on anyone, either angel or human, who might preach a gospel different from his own, and, in the First Letter to the Corinthians, on anyone who does not love the Lord. In later Church usage the phrase 'let him be anathema' invoked a curse on anyone undermining the Christian faith.

Paul's attitude to the well-being of his fellow-Israelites, in his desperation that they should recognise Jesus as Messiah, is similar to that of Moses in Exodus 32:32, when Moses expresses his willingness to be blotted out from the book of life. Moses addresses God: 'If you will only forgive their sin – but if not, blot me out of the book that you have written.' In both cases there is a rhetorical pleading for a people who need God's forgiveness and mercy.

While Paul usually uses the word for 'brothers' of his fellow Christians, here he uses it of those with whom he shares the Jewish faith. 'My own brothers' is translated here as 'my own people'. He stresses that this is a relationship 'according to the flesh'.

v.4 Paul then lists all the prerogatives of Israel, which, to his mind, should have made it easy for them to recognise the Messiah. The first gift to the historical Israel is the 'sonship', translated here as 'adoption'. Moses is instructed to say to Pharaoh: 'Israel is my firstborn son.' (*Exodus 4:22*) In the book of Hosea God says: 'When Israel was a child, I loved him, and out of Egypt I called my son.' (*11:1*)

When Paul speaks of the 'glory' belonging to Israel, he seems to refer to the glory of God accompanying Israel on her journey out of Egypt and through the wilderness, and the glory coming to dwell in the temple in Jerusalem. The 'covenants' are without doubt those made with the patriarchs and with David, by which God confirmed the special calling of Israel. Some ancient manuscripts read 'the covenant' rather than 'the covenants', in which case the covenant with Moses at Sinai would be intended.

The 'giving of the law' and the 'worship' are further gifts of God to Israel. The law or torah given by God at Sinai developed over centuries and gave Israel life. The worship, eventually practised in the temple in Jerusalem, expressed in prayer and sacrifice Israel's unique relationship with God. A further privilege of Israel is the 'promises', particularly those made to the patriarchs, promises of solidarity, land and descendants.

Genesis 15:18 On that day the Lord made a covenant with Abram.

Exodus 2:24 God heard their groaning, and God remembered his covenant with Abraham, Isaac and Jacob.

Exodus 24:8 Moses took the blood and dashed it on the people, and said: 'See the blood of the covenant that the Lord has made with you.'

2 Samuel 23:5 David said: 'He has made with me an everlasting covenant.'

v.5 Having listed so many abstract gifts, Paul now hails the patriarchs themselves. Israel has a history of faith which goes back to the fathers, Abraham, Isaac and Jacob. The gifts listed by Paul are seven in number, which may be intended to point to the completeness of God's gifts to Israel.

Despite receiving so many gifts throughout the history of salvation, Paul knows that the majority of the people of Israel have not accepted this Messiah who comes from Israel 'according to the flesh'. This is the source of his suffering and anguish.

In our translation the Messiah is described as follows: 'who is over all, God blessed for ever'. This part of verse 5 has been the object of intense debate because it refers to Christ as 'God'. In the ancient copies of the New Testament capital letters were always used, and there was no punctuation. The text may equally well be translated as a concluding exclamation in a separate sentence: 'May God who is over all be blessed for ever!' This translation would see these final words as an exclamation in praise of the God who has bestowed such great gifts on the chosen people. Given that in the authentic letters of Paul there is no other reference to Jesus as God, this is probably the correct interpretation.

The Sons of Abraham

vv.6-7 Paul now addresses the question of the fulfilment of the promises of God. How is it that the promises to Israel seem to have failed? Has the word of God failed? Paul explains that God fulfils the promise in the way God chooses.

He introduces what amounts to a new definition of 'Israel'. The true Israel is made up of the children of the promise, not the children of the flesh. He will illustrate this in the following verses by reference to the patriarchs Abraham and Isaac.

'Not all of Abraham's children are his true descendants.' The Book of Genesis tells us of the children of Abraham. His first son, Ishmael, was born of the slave-girl Hagar. In the Letter to the Galatians *(4:23)* Paul explains that Ishmael is not a son of the promise but a son 'according to the flesh'. It is therefore not simply by being a child of Abraham that one is a child of the promise. God chooses who is to be a child of God. Paul then quotes the words of promise from Genesis *(21:12)*: 'It is through Isaac that descendants shall be named for you.' God is not bound to choose all the children of Abraham. God has absolute freedom to show kindness as he wishes.

vv.8-9 Paul makes his point again, and adds another quotation from Genesis *(18:10)*, the words of the messenger announcing the coming birth of Sarah's son, Isaac, the son of the promise.

Close examination of the Book of Genesis reveals that Abraham had many children. Ishmael, born of Hagar, the Egyptian slave-girl, was the ancestor of the Arab people. The story of the birth of Ishmael is reported in Genesis 16. Isaac was of course born of Abraham and his wife Sarah (Genesis 21:2). We also learn in Genesis 25:1-2 that Abraham had six further sons born of Keturah.

In Galatians 3:29 Paul writes: If you belong to Christ, then you are Abraham's offspring, heirs according to the promise.

The Sons of Isaac

v.10 'Nor is that all.' Paul presents another example in order to demonstrate that this is consistently God's way of acting. He makes reference now to the two sons of Isaac, born of Rebecca as twins, the elder brother Esau and the young brother Jacob. The free choice of another son of the promise is shown here too in God's preference for Jacob, the younger son.

v.11 There is an ingenious link here with the fundamental thesis of the Letter to the Romans. Paul explains that the choice of the younger rather than the elder twin was made when they were not yet born, which shows that God's choice was not based on good or bad actions of the individuals concerned, but on God's mercy.

v.12 It was not because of good works, but from the call of God that the younger son became the recipient of the promise. Genesis 25:23, 'the elder shall serve the younger,' is quoted. The choice is made without any regard for human effort.

That the Edomites are the descendants of Esau is illustrated by the extensive genealogies in Genesis chapter 36. The enmity between the descendants of Jacob and the descendants of Esau reached its peak when, many centuries later, after the destruction of the city of Jerusalem in 587 BC and the deportation to Babylon, the Edomites took over the land left behind by the Jews. Ezekiel 35:5 contains these words of judgement on Edom: 'You cherished an ancient enmity, and gave over the people of Israel to the power of the sword at the time of their calamity, at the time of their final punishment.'

A parallel case in Genesis 29:30-31 states that Jacob 'loved Rachel more than Leah'. The text continues: 'When the Lord saw that Leah was hated, he opened her womb; but Rachel was barren.' These verses help us to understand Jesus' words in Luke 14:26: 'Whoever comes to me and does not hate father and mother, wife and children, brothers and sisters, yes, and even life itself, cannot be my disciple.' This is not a command to hate, but to love Jesus more than all others. The parallel words of Jesus in Matthew 10:37 have 'love more'.

The descendants of both Jacob and Esau are ultimately children of Abraham in the physical sense, but no Jew would have maintained that the descendants of Esau, the Edomites, sworn enemies of the Jews for centuries, were members of the people of God. In this way Paul confirms the argument that God's choice is not conditioned by natural descent. Just as God did not choose these children of Abraham, so can God do with the Jews of Paul's day.

v.13 Paul now makes ingenious use of a quotation from the Book of Malachi. At the very beginning of the book of this minor prophet, God affirms his love for Israel, and this love is stressed by contrasting it with his hatred for Edom, the nation descended from Esau. After the traumatic events of the exile and the destruction of Jerusalem the prophet is making clear that God's love for the Jews endures. Paul's quotation from Malachi here, 'I have loved Jacob, but I have hated Esau,' illustrates the special love God has for Israel and once again points to God's freedom to choose whoever he wishes as the recipient of his special care.

One might ask why God 'hates' Esau. This seems to be a dramatic way of emphasising the contrast. The real sense is more like: 'God loved Jacob more than Esau'.

Is God Unjust?

vv.14-15 But doesn't this all mean that God is unjust? 'By no means!' retorts Paul. There must be another way of explaining the situation. He goes on to quote from the Book of Exodus. After the apostasy of worshipping the golden calf, narrated in chapter 32, and Moses' pleas to the Lord for forgiveness, in the subsequent chapter, when Moses asks to see the 'glory' of God (*33:18*), God responds: 'I will make all my goodness pass before you, and will proclaim before you the name, 'The Lord'; and I will be gracious to whom I will be gracious, and will show mercy on whom I will show mercy' (*33:19*).

Paul uses these words of God to summarise what he has explained in verses 6-13, and to counter the claim that God is not just. God shows mercy to whomsoever he wishes. God can therefore call Gentiles as well as Jews to faith in Christ.

v.16 Once again Paul alludes to the main theme of Romans, that salvation does not come by human effort but from the saving justice of God, from God's graciousness and mercy, accepted by faith.

v.17 Paul now seems to complicate matters by a reference to Pharaoh and the Exodus. Paul uses a quotation from Exodus 9:16 and demonstrates how God can use even pagan rulers to proclaim his power and name.

v.18 Paul once again summarises God's behaviour. God has mercy on whomsoever he chooses. What is new here is that he 'hardens the heart of whomever he chooses'. In this Paul takes up a feature of Moses' dealings with Pharaoh. In the early chapters of Exodus it is repeatedly stated that God 'hardens Pharaoh's heart' (*4:21*). This is also presented as Pharaoh's action – 'Pharaoh hardened his heart,' as in 8:15. This might be misunderstood as some kind of predestination to good or evil. The text is best understood as meaning that, when individuals resist the plans of God, God is able to use even this resistance to further his intentions and show his power and his mercy.

The conclusion that Paul seems to imply here is that God can even use the resistance of the Jews to Christ to further his ultimate purpose of salvation, in which God shows mercy to all, the Jewish people and all the nations of the earth.

Dominion of God over pagan rulers can be seen in these words of God:

Isaiah 10:5-6 Ah, Assyria, the rod of my anger, the club in their hands is my fury! Against a godless nation I send him, and against the people of my wrath command him.

Jeremiah 25:9 I am going to send for all the tribes of the north, says the Lord, even for King Nebuchadrezzar of Babylon, my servant.

Isaiah 45:1 Thus says the Lord to his anointed, to Cyrus, whose right hand I have grasped to subdue nations before him.

A later verse of Romans helps here:

Romans 11:11 So I ask, have the Jews stumbled so as to fall? By no means! But through their stumbling salvation has come to the Gentiles, so as to make Israel jealous.

Temple of Ramses II at Abu Simbel, Egypt.

The Word Lives On

In the ferial lectionary our text is part of the semi-continuous reading of the letter spread over four weeks. Romans 9:1-5 is heard on Friday of Week 30 in Year 1. In the Sunday lectionary the same text is set for the nineteenth Sunday in Ordinary Time. It is perhaps owing to the complexity of this chapter that no other verses from it are read in the Liturgy of the Word at Mass.

Pope John Paul II at the Western Wall, Jerusalem.

Live the Word of God

Listen once more to the reading.

Suggestions for reflection and prayer

Do you understand the anguish that Paul feels for his fellow Jews who have not accepted the message and person of Jesus?

❖ Have you ever felt similar anguish when someone close to you has rejected faith in Christ?

❖ Do you value the religious experience of the Jewish people, our fathers and mothers in the faith, and their testimony to God contained in the Bible, or is it largely neglected in your life of faith?

In what sense are Christians 'children of the promise'?

❖ Is the freedom of God in revealing his love in the course of history reflected in human freedom to respond to that love?

❖ Does God really harden people's hearts?

The document of the Second Vatican Council on relations with other religions, entitled Nostra Aetate, reads:

The Church reproves every form of persecution against whomsoever it may be directed. Remembering, then, its common heritage with the Jews and moved not by any political consideration, but solely by the religious motivation of Christian charity, it deplores all hatreds, persecutions, and displays of anti-semitism levelled at any time or from any source against the Jews. The Church always held and continues to hold that Christ out of infinite love freely underwent suffering and death because of the sins of all, so that all might attain salvation. It is the duty of the Church, therefore, in its preaching to proclaim the cross of Christ as the sign of God's universal love and the source of all grace. (4)

An Unenlightened Zeal

Hear the Word of God

Romans 10:1-18

Brothers and sisters, my heart's desire and prayer to God for them is that they may be saved. [2] I can testify that they have a zeal for God, but it is not enlightened. [3] For, being ignorant of the righteousness that comes from God, and seeking to establish their own, they have not submitted to God's righteousness. [4] For Christ is the end of the law so that there may be righteousness for everyone who believes.

[5] Moses writes concerning the righteousness that comes from the law, that 'the person who does these things will live by them.' [6] But the righteousness that comes from faith says, 'Do not say in your heart, "Who will ascend into heaven?" ' (that is, to bring Christ down) 7 'or "Who will descend into the abyss?" ' (that is, to bring Christ up from the dead). [8] But what does it say?

'The word is near you, on your lips and in your heart' (that is, the word of faith that we proclaim); [9] because if you confess with your lips that Jesus is Lord and believe in your heart that God raised him from the dead, you will be saved. [10] For one believes with the heart and so is justified, and one confesses with the mouth and so is saved. [11] The scripture says, 'No one who believes in him will be put to shame.' [12] For there is no distinction between Jew and Greek; the same Lord is Lord of all and is generous to all who call on him. [13] For, 'Everyone who calls on the name of the Lord shall be saved.'

[14] But how are they to call on one in whom they have not believed? And how are they to believe in one of whom they have never heard? And how are they to hear without someone to proclaim him? [15] And how are they to proclaim him unless they are sent? As it is written, 'How beautiful are the feet of those who bring good news!' [16] But not all have obeyed the good news; for Isaiah says, 'Lord, who has believed our message?' [17] So faith comes from what is heard, and what is heard comes through the word of Christ.

[18] But, I ask, have they not heard? Indeed they have; for 'Their voice has gone out to all the earth, and their words to the ends of the world.'

Opposite: Easter Island Moai Statues.

Understand the Word of God

This session will explore:

❖ the zeal of the Jewish people

❖ justification by deeds or by faith

❖ the crucial role of the preacher

Setting in the Letter

We continue with another section from Paul's lengthy consideration of the situation of the Jewish people after the coming of Christ in Romans 9-11. In chapter 9 he stressed the absolute freedom of God to show mercy to those whom he chooses, whether Jew or Gentile. In the final verses of the chapter Paul considered the human response to God. In verses 30-33 he reintroduced the fundamental theme of the letter, explaining that the Gentiles attained righteousness through faith, whereas Israel, intent on achieving righteousness by their own efforts to obey the law, failed to reach it.

Paul ended chapter 9 with a combined quotation from Isaiah chapters 8 and 28: 'See, I am laying in Sion a stone that will make people stumble.' This text is frequently used by Christian writers to refer to the need for faith. The human response to the call of faith continues as the theme in chapter 10.

1 Peter 2:6-8 combines the same passages about the stone (from Isaiah 8:14-15 and 28:16) with a quotation from Psalm 118:22. In Mark 12:10 Jesus ends the parable of the wicked tenants by quoting the same passage from the psalm: 'The stone that the builders rejected has become the cornerstone.' The same text is used by Peter in his address to the Sanhedrin in Acts 4:11. Jesus, the precious corner-stone, invites a decision and the commitment of faith.

What Kind of Text?

Chapter 10 opens, as did chapter 9, with a reference to Paul's feelings for his Jewish brothers and sisters. Paul is desperate that they should be saved but claims that their zeal for God is 'not enlightened'.

Once again in this complex passage Paul uses frequent quotations from the Scriptures, this time in order to draw a comparison between the righteousness which comes from the law and the righteousness which comes from faith (verses 5-13).

A section of diatribe then follows with frequent rhetorical questions and several quotations from the Scriptures. All in all, the text is very similar in style to chapter 9. The focus, however, is different: Paul balances his statements in chapter 9 about the absolute freedom of God with consideration of the human response to God's call.

Scroll of Hebrew Scripture.

Commentary: verse by verse reading

The End of the Law

v.1 Paul repeats in simpler fashion what he had said at the beginning of chapter 9. In 9:3 he said that he would willingly be 'accursed and cut off from Christ' if this would save his own people. Here Paul speaks of the desire of his heart and his prayer to God that they may be saved. Paul was clear from the start of the letter that 'the gospel is the power of God for salvation to everyone who has faith, to the Jew first and also to the Greek' (*1:16*).

In the first Book of Maccabees, which tells of the persecution of the Jewish faith by the Hellenistic rulers of Palestine in the second century BC, Mattathias, the leader of the Jewish revolt, is described as 'burning with zeal for the law' (1:26). He summons followers with the words: 'Let everyone who is zealous for the law and supports the covenant come with me!' (1:27)

v.2 Paul knows that the Jews have 'a zeal for God'. In Galatians 1:14 he had described himself as 'far more zealous for the traditions of my ancestors' than his contemporaries. But in Paul's opinion their zeal is 'not enlightened'. A literal translation reads that their zeal is 'not according to knowledge', using the Greek word *epignosis*, which is found again in Colossians 2:2 of 'the knowledge of the mystery of God, namely Christ'. The Jews, despite their zeal, are not aware of the gifts brought by Christ.

v.3 The Jews in fact are not aware of God's 'justice'. The Greek word *dikaiosune*, which we encountered for the first time in Romans 1:17, and then frequently in chapter 3, reappears. God's 'justice' or 'righteousness' includes his mercy to those who fail. This is what the Jews have not appreciated. Justification by faith in Jesus Christ eludes them. They rely instead on their own justification, their own righteousness through obeying the law.

v.4 'Christ is the end of the law.' Paul uses the Greek word *telos* for 'end'. Various interpretations have been proposed. Christ could be understood as bringing the law to an end in the sense of abolishing the law. It seems more likely that we should understand Christ as the 'goal' towards which the law was leading.

This would be in harmony with Christ's statement in Matthew's Sermon on the Mount: 'Do not think that I have come to abolish the law and the prophets; I have come not to abolish them but to bring them to fulfilment' (*Matthew 5:17*). Paul seems to have a similar sense that the law is a preparation for Christ. In Romans 3:31 he asked the question, 'Do we then overthrow the law by this faith?' and gave the answer, 'By no means! On the contrary, we uphold the law.' Later, in Romans 13:10, Paul will write that 'love is the fulfilment of the law'. Justification by faith in Christ is the goal towards which the law pointed, and is now available for all.

St Ambrose of Milan teaches:

Christ is the end of the law, not in the sense of a deficiency, but in the sense of the fullness of the Law: a fullness which is achieved in Christ, since he came not to abolish the Law but to bring it to fulfilment. In the same way that there is an Old Testament, but all truth is in the New Testament, so it is for the Law: what was given through Moses is a figure of the true law. Therefore, the Mosaic Law is an image of the truth. (In Psalmum CXVIII Expositio, Sermo 18, 37)

From the Catechism of the Catholic Church:

The moral law finds its fullness and its unity in Christ. Jesus Christ is in person the way of perfection. He is the end of the law, for only he teaches and bestows the justice of God. (1953)

This hill is a suggested location of the Sermon on the Mount. Once known as Mt. Eremos, this hill is located between Capernaum and Tabgha and is just above the 'Cove of the Sower.' This spacious hillside provides much room for crowds to gather.

Two Kinds of Righteousness

v.5 Paul now embarks on the interpretation of two passages of Scripture in order to illustrate the difference between the righteousness which comes from the law and the righteousness which comes from faith. He first quotes Leviticus 18:5, which reads 'the one who does these things will live by them'. This text is easily understood as pointing to justification by obedience to the law. Paul suggests that this is what Moses proposed and what Moses stands for. In this view fidelity to the letter of the law guarantees life.

vv.6-8 In order to illustrate the second kind of righteousness, the righteousness which comes from faith, Paul turns to a text of Deuteronomy, which allows him to consider the interior dispositions of the person rather than the simple external observation of the law.

Paul's use of the text of Deuteronomy 30:11-14 is far from simple. In order to understand it we need to recognise that he has inserted two phrases pointing to Christ: 'that is, to bring Christ down' and 'that is, to bring Christ up from the dead'. If we omit the additions, the text of Deuteronomy used by Paul reads: 'Do not say in your heart: Who will ascend into heaven? Or who will descend into the abyss?' The question being asked is where is true teaching, where is the word of God to be found. The answer is given: 'The word is near you, on your lips and in your heart.'

The full text of Deuteronomy 30:11-14 in the Hebrew Bible runs as follows:

Surely, this commandment that I am commanding you today is not too hard for you, nor is it too far away. It is not in heaven, that you should say, 'Who will go up to heaven for us, and get it for us so that we may hear it and observe it?' Neither is it beyond the sea, that you should say, 'Who will cross to the other side of the sea for us, and get it for us so that we may hear it and observe it?' No, the word is very near to you; it is in your mouth and in your heart for you to observe.

Moses with the Tablets of the Law by Claude Vignon.

Helpfully, in the New Revised Standard Version text we are using, Paul's christological additions are given in brackets. Paul is creating a midrash of the text of Deuteronomy. He edits the text to show how it sheds light on Christian faith. This is a new way of reading the text, what scholars sometimes call a 're-reading' of the passage, and is designed to show its relevance to Christianity. In its original form Deuteronomy 30:11-14 maintains that true teaching has been given to Israel and that it is to be found, not far away, but on the lips and in the hearts of the people. By his editing of the text, Paul suggests that the fullness of true teaching is found in Christ, and that it is by faith in him that salvation can be reached. The 'word' is 'the word of faith that we proclaim'.

The use of midrash was common among the Jews of this period. The Hebrew word literally means 'searching'. Essentially it was an attempt to interpret the biblical text in such a way that it spoke to the contemporary situation of the believer.

The Christian Confession of Faith

vv.9-10 Paul now considers what should be on the lips and in the heart of Christians. 'Jesus is Lord' is an early profession of faith, which points to Christ's triumph and to his divinity. With its use of the Greek word *kurios* it is a direct challenge to the Roman emperor and his 'lordship'. In 1 Corinthians 12:3 Paul writes: 'No one can say "Jesus is Lord" except by the Holy Spirit.'

In the 'Martyrdom of Saint Polycarp' (8:2) it is narrated that, while Polycarp, the eighty-six year old bishop of Smyrna in Asia Minor in the second century, is being led to his death, he is asked: 'Why is it so wrong to save yourself by saying "Caesar is Lord", making a sacrifice, and so on?' Polycarp's reply is: 'I am not about to do what you advise.'

In addition to the declaration of the lips that 'Jesus is Lord', Paul also expects Christians to believe in their hearts that God raised him from the dead. He writes in 1 Corinthians 15:17: 'If Christ has not been raised, your faith is futile and you are still in your sins.' In this presentation of the essentials of Christian faith, Paul is still alluding to the text of Deuteronomy with its reference to 'the word' on the lips and in the heart. For Paul this word is the good news of Christ. This faith, believed and confessed, leads to justification and salvation.

St Ambrose writes:

With these twin trumpets of heart and mouth we arrive at that holy land, the grace of resurrection. So let them always sound together in harmony for us, that we may always hear the voice of God. Let the utterances of the angels and prophets arouse us and move us to hasten to higher things. (On the Death of his Brother Satyrus 21.112)

v.11 Paul uses further texts to illustrate this. Firstly he repeats the final words of chapter 9, which were part of a quotation from Isaiah 28. He omits all reference to the stone laid in Sion and uses only the final words about faith.

vv.12-13 Paul stresses once again that there is no distinction between Jew and Greek, as he explained in Romans 3:22-23. He refers again to Jesus, the *kurios*, and describes him as 'Lord of all', once more emphasising that all people, Jews and Gentiles, are under his lordship.

He describes the Lord Jesus as 'generous' to all who call on him. The word 'generous' here can be translated more literally as 'showering riches on'. Finally, Paul adds a quotation from the prophet Joel (3:5/2:32): 'Everyone who calls on the name of the Lord shall be saved.' The same text is quoted by Peter during the Pentecost speech in Acts 2:21.

Christian Preaching

v.14 While Romans 9 had stressed the absolute freedom of God to offer mercy to whomsoever he chooses, in this chapter Paul is considering the human response to God's call. Human beings can accept or reject the message of the gospel. In a series of rhetorical questions he raises the possibility that maybe the message has not been accepted because it has not been proclaimed. There will be no believing without hearing the message, and no hearing the message without it being first proclaimed.

v.15 Paul takes the argument further by saying that heralds of the message need to be sent (Greek *apostellein*). Christian preachers need to take up their apostolic task. Paul insisted that he was 'called to be an apostle, set apart for the gospel of God' (*Romans 1:1*).

'How beautiful are the feet of those who bring good news!' The quotation from Isaiah 52:17 speaks of those sent to proclaim a message of liberation. In the second part of the book of the prophet Isaiah there is considerable emphasis on the good news brought to the exiles that their return home is imminent. The good news of the return to Sion prepares for the good news of Jesus Christ.

v.16 So the heralds have been sent, and the good news has been proclaimed, but not all have believed. Paul quotes Isaiah 53:1, a verse from the fourth Song of the Servant, which he takes in isolation from its context. The question is rhetorical. The implication is that not many have believed. The Christian message has been rejected, just as that of the prophet was.

vv.17-18 Paul's first words here have become something of a slogan: *fides ex auditu* – faith comes from hearing, and from hearing the word of Christ. In verse 18 Paul returns to his rhetorical questions. He employs Psalm 19, one of the psalms in praise of God the creator, to give an answer to the question, 'have they not heard?' The psalm has the heavens speak out in praise of God's power. 'Their voice goes forth to all the earth.' Paul transfers the verse to the proclamation of the heralds of the gospels, who brought the apostolic preaching to the ends of the earth.

In other words, as Paul will explain in the concluding verses of the chapter, the message has been preached but many have remained 'disobedient and defiant' (*10:21*). God has not simply abandoned his people. The gospel message has gone out to them, but there are many who have refused to listen.

At this stage it may seem that Paul has no hope for those who have rejected the gospel. But Paul has not finished. In chapter 11, the final chapter of this sermon on the situation of the Jews, Paul will speak of the future hope of Israel.

The Songs of the Servant are four poems found in the second part of the book of Isaiah. They speak of a servant called to bring justice to the nations. In so doing he is persecuted and eventually gives his life as a ransom. The songs are found in chapters 42, 49, 50 and 52-53 of the Book of Isaiah. They are read at Mass during Holy Week, since they point to Jesus and to his suffering and death.

No one – no individual and no community – can proclaim the Gospel to himself. 'Faith comes from what is heard.' No one can give himself the mandate and the mission to proclaim the Gospel. The one sent by the Lord does not speak and act on his own authority, but by virtue of Christ's authority. (Catechism of the Catholic Church 875)

Handel's 'Messiah' includes the soprano aria 'How Beautiful are the feet' from Romans 10.

The Word Lives On

Although Romans chapter 10 does not appear at all in the ferial lectionary, verses 8-13 are read on the 1st Sunday of Lent in Year C. With their clear reference to the Christian confession of faith they can also be used at Baptisms of adults.

Romans 10:9-18 is the first reading for the Feast of St Andrew the Apostle (30th November), and may also be read at Masses for Evangelisation. In both cases the Responsorial Psalm is Psalm 19, which was quoted by Paul at the end of the text. The response to the psalm is 'Their span goes forth through all the earth.'

Whenever a deacon is to read the gospel at Mass, the priest or bishop gives him a blessing with the words: 'The Lord be in your heart and on your lips that you may worthily proclaim his holy gospel, in the name of the Father, and of the Son, and of the Holy Spirit.'

Statue of St Andrew, at the base of the four pillars supporting the dome, St Peter's Basilica, Vatican, Rome.

Live the Word of God

Listen once more to the reading.

Suggestions for reflection and prayer

Paul maintains that the zeal of his Jewish brothers and sisters is 'not enlightened'.

❖ Can I think of any aspect of my life to which a similar criticism might apply?

Is the faith of the gospel really on my lips and in my heart?

❖ Is it there day by day and at all times?

❖ Or are there times when my faith is stifled and silenced amid the raised voices of daily life?

The Lord is generous to all who call on him.

❖ Do I imitate the Lord's generosity in my dealings with others?

Have I accepted the vocation given me by God?

❖ Am I willing to bring the good news to all the earth?

❖ Do I have the necessary courage and compassion?

❖ Do I consider all people to be children of God, even those who do not know God?

In the encyclical letter 'Redemptoris Missio', promulgated in 1990, Pope John Paul II wrote:

While respecting the beliefs and sensitivities of all, we must first clearly affirm our faith in Christ, the one Saviour of mankind, a faith we have received as a gift from on high, not as a result of any merit of our own. We say with Paul, "I am not ashamed of the Gospel: it is the power of God for salvation to everyone who has faith" (Rom 1:16). Christian martyrs of all times - including our own - have given and continue to give their lives in order to bear witness to this faith, in the conviction that every human being needs Jesus Christ, who has conquered sin and death and reconciled mankind to God. (11)

All Israel will be Saved

Hear the Word of God

Romans 11:13-32

[13] Now I am speaking to you Gentiles. Inasmuch then as I am an apostle to the Gentiles, I glorify my ministry [14] in order to make my own people jealous, and thus save some of them. [15] For if their rejection is the reconciliation of the world, what will their acceptance be but life from the dead! [16] If the part of the dough offered as first fruits is holy, then the whole batch is holy; and if the root is holy, then the branches also are holy.

[17] But if some of the branches were broken off, and you, a wild olive shoot, were grafted in their place to share the rich root of the olive tree, [18] do not vaunt yourselves over the branches. If you do vaunt yourselves, remember that it is not you that support the root, but the root that supports you. [19] You will say, 'Branches were broken off so that I might be grafted in.' [20] That is true. They were broken off because of their unbelief, but you stand only through faith. So do not become proud, but stand in awe. [21] For if God did not spare the natural branches, perhaps he will not spare you. [22] Note then the kindness and the severity of God: severity towards those who have fallen, but God's kindness towards you, provided you continue in his kindness; otherwise you also will be cut off. [23] And even those of Israel, if they do not persist in unbelief, will be grafted in, for God has the power to graft them in again. [24] For if you have been cut from what is by nature a wild olive tree and grafted, contrary to nature, into a cultivated olive tree, how much more will these natural branches be grafted back into their own olive tree.

[25] So that you may not claim to be wiser than you are, brothers and sisters, I want you to understand this mystery: a hardening has come upon part of Israel, until the full number of the Gentiles has come in. [26] And so all Israel will be saved; as it is written, 'Out of Zion will come the Deliverer; he will banish ungodliness from Jacob.' [27] 'And this is my covenant with them, when I take away their sins.'

[28] As regards the gospel they are enemies of God for your sake; but as regards election they are beloved, for the sake of their ancestors; [29] for the gifts and the calling of God are irrevocable. [30] Just as you were once disobedient to God but have now received mercy because of their disobedience, [31] so they have now been disobedient in order that, by the mercy shown to you, they too may now receive mercy. [32] For God has imprisoned all in disobedience so that he may be merciful to all.

Opposite: St Paul mosaic in Baptistery of the Arians, Ravenna.

Understand the Word of God

This session will explore:

- ✤ salvation offered to the Gentiles
- ✤ the image of the olive tree
- ✤ God's fidelity to Israel

Setting in the Letter

This is our final passage from Paul's extended treatment of the situation of the Jewish people after the coming of Christ, which covers Romans chapters 9-11. Paul began in chapter 9 by explaining the freedom of God in showing mercy to those whom he chooses, whether they are Jew or Gentile. In chapter 10 Paul considered the response of the Jews to God's call. They pursued righteousness by the works of the law, and did not embrace the free gift of justification through faith in Christ. Paul ended chapter 10 by quoting from Isaiah 65:2 which describes the Jews as 'a disobedient and defiant people'.

In chapter 11 Paul will explain that this disbelief and rejection of the gospel message does not apply to all Jews, and that it is only temporary. Furthermore, it is providential. In the end 'all Israel will be saved' (verse 26). After the passage we are considering, Paul concludes the chapter with a hymn to the merciful goodness of God in 11:33-36.

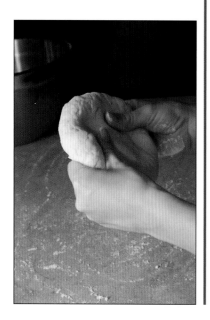

Ancient olive tree.

What Kind of Text?

Romans 11:13-32 is far less dominated by quotations from the Old Testament than the previous chapters were. The most striking feature in these verses is the use of images, firstly the image of the dough, which is briefly mentioned, and then, in a much more developed way, the image of the olive tree with its ancient and venerable root, and its branches, some old ones lopped off and some new ones grafted on. The olive tree now stands for all those who believe in Christ, whatever their origin.

Commentary: verse by verse reading

Two Images

Galatians 2:8 He who worked through Peter making him an apostle to the circumcised also worked through me in sending me to the Gentiles.

v.13 It is as if Paul at this stage reminds himself that he is speaking to Christians who are mostly converts from paganism. He has become so absorbed in the Jewish question that he now explicitly recalls that he is writing to Gentiles, and that his mission is to be 'apostle of the Gentiles'. At the beginning of the letter Paul had addressed the Romans as Gentiles 'called to belong to Jesus Christ' (1:6).

v.14 Paul suggests that his service as apostle to the Gentiles should 'make my own people jealous, and thus save some of them'. We are aware again of the depth of feeling Paul has for those he actually calls 'my own flesh' (Greek *mou ten sarka*). As in 9:2-3, his concern for his Jewish brothers and sisters seems to override all else. His ultimate goal, as always, is the salvation of others.

Paul speaks elsewhere of reconciliation:

Romans 5:10 For if while we were enemies, we were reconciled to God through the death of his Son, much more surely, having been reconciled, will we be saved by his life.

2 Corinthians 5:19 In Christ God was reconciling the world to himself, not counting their trespasses against them, and entrusting the message of reconciliation to us.

v.15 What does Paul mean by 'their rejection' and 'their acceptance'? In English this seems to mean that the Jews have been rejected and will subsequently be accepted again. But Paul has already ruled this out in 11:1, where he wrote: 'Has God then rejected his people? By no means!' The Greek text seems to refer rather to their present rejection of the gospel, and their future acceptance of it. This makes much more sense. The rejection of the gospel by the Jews led to the preaching to the nations and the consequent reconciliation of the nations to God. The subsequent acceptance of the gospel by the Jewish people will be for them like 'life from the dead'.

Numbers 15:20: 'From the first batch of dough you shall present a loaf as a donation; you shall present it just as you present a donation from the threshing floor. Throughout your generations you shall give to the Lord a donation from the first of your batch of dough.'

v.16 In this verse Paul introduces two metaphors. He speaks first of the first-fruits (Greek *aparche*). In Numbers 15:20 Israel is commanded to present to God an offering from the first batch of dough after the harvest. It was understood that this offering to God made the rest of the food holy.

The second metaphor, the root and branches of the olive tree, will be extensively developed in the coming verses. The two images have this in common, that a part that is holy brings holiness to the rest. The first batch of dough offered to God makes the rest holy and individual branches become holy through the holiness of the root.

In the prophets we see the origins of the second metaphor of the olive tree. In Hosea 14:6 God says of Israel: 'His shoots shall spread out; his beauty shall be like the olive tree, and his fragrance like that of Lebanon.' In Jeremiah 11:16 the prophet speaks to Judah and Jerusalem, the remnant of the people in his day: 'The Lord once called you, "A green olive tree, fair with goodly fruit"; but with the roar of a great tempest he will set fire to it, and its branches will be consumed.' Israel, often compared to a vine as in Isaiah 5:1-7, is here compared to an olive tree, with its root and branches.

Towards the end of Psalm 52 the psalmist uses the image of the olive tree to speak of his love for the temple of God: But I am like a green olive tree in the house of God. I trust in the steadfast love of God forever and ever.

v.17 Paul, however, introduces an entirely new angle to the metaphor by speaking of the removal of old branches and the grafting of new branches on to the old stock. The branches which have been broken off are individual Jews who have not accepted the gospel. The new branches, 'wild olive shoots', are Gentiles who have been grafted on to the original tree.

The wild olive shoot becomes a 'sharer', literally 'in communion together' (Greek *sugkoinonos*), in the richness of the old tree. The metaphor proclaims that Gentiles are brought into communion with the rich blessings granted to Abraham and his descendants.

It seems that the more normal method of grafting would be to graft branches from an older tree onto a young olive plant. Nevertheless, the method of grafting new branches onto an old stock is attested in ancient times by the Roman writer, Lucius Junius Moderatus Columella. A contemporary of Paul, he wrote a volume on agriculture (De re rustica) in which is included a section on growing olive trees.

v.18 The newly arrived Gentile Christians, symbolized by the new branches which take the place of the branches which have been broken off, have no reason to boast, to 'vaunt themselves' or feel superior (Greek *katakauchomai*). Paul constantly urges the Christians of Rome not to boast (Greek *kauchomai*), for they have received salvation as a free gift from God, and not as a result of their own efforts.

The Gentile Christians are reminded that they depend on the ancient root of Israel, which remains the bringer of life for both Jew and Gentile. There is no warrant for them to feel superior to the branches which have been removed.

Romans 3:27 Then what becomes of boasting? It is excluded. By what law? By that of works? No, but by the law of faith.

Romans 5:2-3 We boast in our hope of sharing the glory of God. And not only that, but we also boast in our sufferings.

Romans 5:11 But more than that, we even boast in God through our Lord Jesus Christ, through whom we have now received reconciliation.

vv.19-20 Paul continues to warn the Gentile Christians about self-importance and complacency. The Gentiles have nothing to be proud of since they have not achieved salvation by their works but have received a gift from God, to which they have responded by faith in Jesus Christ. They are warned not to be proud, literally not to 'think haughty things', but rather to have a godly fear. In Romans 12:16, in a more general context, Paul will use the same phrase: 'Do not be haughty, but associate with the lowly.'

v.21 This is Paul's starkest warning. The branches of the ancient olive tree were lopped off due to lack of faith. The Gentile Christians, the new branches grafted on to the ancient olive tree, may still not reach salvation if in their pride and complacency they themselves lose faith.

The Kindness and Severity of God

v.22 Paul uses two unusual words to speak of the qualities of God. To speak of God's kindness he uses the Greek word *chrestotes*. Paul used the expression before in Romans 2:4, when he wrote: 'Or do you despise the riches of God's kindness and forbearance and patience?' In the Letter to Titus 3:4 the word is paired with *philanthropia*, God's 'love of human beings'. This kindness is shown in admitting both Jew and Gentile to salvation through faith.

Titus 3:4-5 When the kindness and love of God our Saviour appeared, he saved us, not because of any works of righteousness that we had done, but according to his mercy.

Paul writes of God's severity, using the Greek word *apotomia*. This is the only use of the word in the New Testament, but the Book of Wisdom *(6:5)* addresses kings and rulers as follows: 'God will come upon you terribly and swiftly, because severe judgment falls on those in high places.' This severity of God, Paul writes, is reserved for those who 'have fallen' through unbelief. The Gentiles are encouraged to remain in the kindness of God lest they be cut off too.

v.23 There can be change too for the Jews who have not believed, if they abandon their unbelief. God has the power to graft them back again, for God can graft old branches back onto the old stock.

v.24 Paul explains that God will accept back the Jews who initially rejected faith in Christ. They will naturally find their home again in the ancient olive tree, to which they originally belonged. Israel's rejection of the gospel and of faith in Christ will come to an end.

The Mystery Explained

v.25 Paul insists that what he is talking of here is a 'mystery'. It is something which comes from the merciful love of God. In the Letter to the Ephesians 3:3-5 Paul uses the same term *musterion* in similar fashion to speak of God's way of offering salvation to all.

Awareness of this mystery is true wisdom, a wisdom that comes from God. But Paul lays particular emphasis on one dimension of this mystery of salvation. The unbelief of Israel will last 'until the full number of the Gentiles has come in'. Paul uses the Greek word *pleroma*, which signifies 'fullness'. In 11:12 he used it of the Jews, and here he uses it of the Gentiles. There is a sense of God's plan of salvation coming to its fulfilment. The partial and temporary hardening of heart by Israel is a particular aspect of the mystery now made known.

Ephesians 3:5-6 In former generations this mystery was not made known to humankind, as it has now been revealed to his holy apostles and prophets by the Spirit: that is, the Gentiles have become fellow heirs, members of the same body, and sharers in the promise in Christ Jesus through the gospel.

v.26 'And so all Israel will be saved.' This crucial sentence has been the object of much discussion. How is Israel to be saved? For Paul the salvation of everyone, whether Jew or Gentile, comes through Christ. The gospel, after all, is 'the power of God for salvation to everyone who has faith, to the Jew first and also to the Greek' (*1:16*). Paul cannot conceive of salvation without Christ. 'All Israel' complements the 'full number of the Gentiles' mentioned in the previous verse.

St Theodoret of Cyr, fifth century bishop and scholar, gives a different definition of 'all Israel':

'All Israel' means all those who believe, whether they are Jews, who have a natural relationship to Israel, or Gentiles, who are related to Israel by faith. (Interpretation of the Letter to the Romans)

Paul undergirds this idea with quotations from Scripture. The first is from Isaiah 59:20-21. In this third part of the Book of Isaiah there is a focus on definitive salvation. The 'deliverer' for Paul is clearly Christ Jesus.

v.27 Paul then alludes to Jeremiah 31:33-34, where, speaking of a new covenant with Israel, God promises the forgiveness of sin. Paul sees how this text in particular can speak to the contemporary situation of Israel after the coming of Christ. The focus of salvation is on the merciful forgiveness of God.

Jeremiah 31:33-34

This is the covenant that I will make with the house of Israel after those days, says the Lord: I will put my law within them, and I will write it on their hearts; and I will be their God, and they shall be my people. No longer shall they teach one another, or say to each other, "Know the Lord", for they shall all know me, from the least of them to the greatest, says the Lord; for I will forgive their iniquity, and remember their sin no more.

St John Chrysostom comments:

God's covenant will be fulfilled not when they are circumcised, nor when they do the other deeds of the law, but when they obtain forgiveness of sins. If this has been promised but has not yet happened in their case, nor have they enjoyed the forgiveness of sins in baptism, nevertheless it will certainly come to pass. (Homilies on Romans 19)

v.28 In a further effort to explain the mystery, and summarise what he has been saying, Paul refers to the people of Israel as both 'enemies' and 'beloved'. The Jews have been ranked as enemies owing to their rejection of the gospel 'for the sake of the Gentiles', but they always remain beloved as God's chosen people 'for the sake of the patriarchs'. Paul shows here his deep appreciation of the role of the chosen people from the time of Abraham. His teaching shows how misguided is the denigration of the ancient people of God which has been so common in Christianity throughout the centuries. Nothing can change the status of the Jewish people as beloved in the eyes of God, even if, temporarily and providentially, they have rejected the gospel.

Above right: The Prophet Jeremiah, Sistine Chapel Ceiling.

v.29 Paul spells out the theological principle which underpins his teaching: God is faithful and true. In 1 Corinthians 1:9 Paul writes: 'God is faithful; by him you were called into the fellowship of his Son, Jesus Christ our Lord.' Later in the same letter, in 10:13, he says: 'God is faithful, and he will not let you be tested beyond your strength.' Here again Paul stresses the constancy of God. God never revokes his gifts and calling. Once bestowed, they are not taken back.

vv.30-31 These two verses are cleverly structured, with repeated reference to 'disobedience' and to 'mercy'. In the Greek original there is even a similarity in the sound of the words paired up here. The final emphasis is not on disobedience but on mercy, for this is God's final purpose.

v.32 This verse sums up the mystery of which Paul has been speaking in a few words. God is able to use the disobedience of both Gentile and Jew in order to show mercy. In this way Paul shows God's sovereignty without undermining human free will. God shows mercy to all through Jesus Christ. These final reflections bring Paul's consideration of this complex issue to an end. In the final verses of the chapter (verses 33-36) he will sing the praises of the wisdom of God.

Paul concludes with an exultant hymn of praise:

O the depth of the riches and wisdom and knowledge of God! How unsearchable are his judgments and how inscrutable his ways! For who has known the mind of the Lord? Or who has been his counsellor? Or who has given a gift to him, to receive a gift in return? For from him and through him and to him are all things. To him be the glory for ever. Amen. (11:33-36)

St Paul's outside the walls, Rome, the burial site of St Paul.

St Cyril of Jerusalem draws a connection between the image of the olive tree in Romans 11 and the baptism his converts have received:

When you were stripped you were anointed with exorcised olive oil, from the topmost hairs of your head to the soles of your feet, and became partakers of the good olive tree, Jesus Christ. Cuttings from the wild olive tree, you were grafted into the good olive tree and became partakers of the richness of the true olive tree. (Mystagogical Lectures 2.3)

The Word Lives On

On the Twentieth Sunday in Ordinary Time in Year A we hear Romans 11:13-15 and 29-32 as the second reading at Mass. In the ferial lectionary on Saturday of the thirtieth week in Year 1 selected verses from Romans 11 are read, and on Monday of the thirty-first week we hear the concluding verses of the chapter, verses 29-36.

Live the Word of God

Suggestions for reflection and prayer

Paul describes Israel as an ancient olive tree, which provides strength to its branches, old and new.

❖ What is my attitude to the Jewish heritage of Christianity?

❖ Do I treasure the Scriptures of the Old Testament?

❖ Do I value the Jewish religion and culture of Jesus and the early Christians?

The ancient olive tree is ready to receive the new branches of the Gentiles.

❖ What is my attitude to those from other lands who live in our midst?

❖ Am I prejudiced against them, or do I welcome them into the community?

How do I experience the 'kindness and severity' of God?

❖ Is my life of faith a loving response to the God of love, or fearful compliance to a God of commandments and punishment?

Paul speaks of the 'mystery' of God's dealings with Jews and Gentiles.

❖ Am I open to the fact that I cannot grasp the plan of God in its totality?

God's gifts to us and his calling are 'irrevocable'.

❖ Am I faithful in my response to the faithfulness of God?

The Catechism of the Catholic Church quotes from the Council document on the Church (Lumen Gentium) as follows:

The Church is a cultivated field, the tillage of God. On that land the ancient olive tree grows whose holy roots were the prophets and in which the reconciliation of Jews and Gentiles has been brought about and will be brought about again. That land, like a choice vineyard, has been planted by the heavenly cultivator. (755)

Living the Christian Life

Hear the Word of God

Romans 12:1-21

I appeal to you therefore, brothers and sisters, by the mercies of God, to present your bodies as a living sacrifice, holy and acceptable to God, which is your spiritual worship. [2] Do not be conformed to this world, but be transformed by the renewing of your minds, so that you may discern what is the will of God—what is good and acceptable and perfect.

[3] For by the grace given to me I say to everyone among you not to think of yourself more highly than you ought to think, but to think with sober judgement, each according to the measure of faith that God has assigned. [4] For as in one body we have many members, and not all the members have the same function, [5] so we, who are many, are one body in Christ, and individually we are members one of another. [6] We have gifts that differ according to the grace given to us: prophecy, in proportion to faith; [7] ministry, in ministering; the teacher, in teaching; [8] the exhorter, in exhortation; the giver, in generosity; the leader, in diligence; the compassionate, in cheerfulness.

[9] Let love be genuine; hate what is evil, hold fast to what is good; [10] love one another with mutual affection; outdo one another in showing honour. [11] Do not lag in zeal, be ardent in spirit, serve the Lord. [12] Rejoice in hope, be patient in suffering, persevere in prayer. [13] Contribute to the needs of the saints; extend hospitality to strangers.

[14] Bless those who persecute you; bless and do not curse them. [15] Rejoice with those who rejoice, weep with those who weep. [16] Live in harmony with one another; do not be haughty, but associate with the lowly; do not claim to be wiser than you are. [17] Do not repay anyone evil for evil, but take thought for what is noble in the sight of all. [18] If it is possible, so far as it depends on you, live peaceably with all. [19] Beloved, never avenge yourselves, but leave room for the wrath of God; for it is written, 'Vengeance is mine, I will repay, says the Lord.' [20] No, 'if your enemies are hungry, feed them; if they are thirsty, give them something to drink; for by doing this you will heap burning coals on their heads.' [21] Do not be overcome by evil, but overcome evil with good.

Opposite: Ss Peter and Paul Embracing, Byzantine School.

Understand the Word of God

This session will explore:
- ❖ the self-sacrifice of the Christian
- ❖ Paul's catalogue of moral teaching
- ❖ similarities with the teaching of Jesus

Setting in the Letter

We have reached the final chapters of the Letter to the Romans. Having worked through Paul's complex presentation of fundamental topics of Christian faith, such as justification, life in the Spirit, and the Jewish question, we enter into a somewhat easier and lighter section which spells out the implications of faith in the daily life of the Christian.

What Kind of Text?

The opening words of the chapter make quite clear that these verses are an exhortation to the Christians of Rome to live their Christian lives to the full. Romans 12-15 spells out some of the practical demands of life as a Christian justified by faith in Jesus Christ. With phrases such as 'I appeal to you', 'do not be conformed', 'be transformed' Paul presents a direct challenge to them, even though he has never met them, and never visited Rome.

Characteristic of this passage is a wide variety of moral exhortations. Verses 9-21 contain an extraordinarily lengthy list of counsels for the everyday behaviour of the Christian. This chapter is not, however, a systematic treatment of the moral requirements of Christianity but a rather rambling selection of the practical demands of the life of love, lived for the common good.

Christian agape, detail from sarcophagus lid.

Commentary: verse by verse reading

Offer Your Lives to God

v.1 Paul addresses the Roman Christians simply as 'brothers', as he did for the first time in the first chapter of Romans (*1:13*). He appeals to them 'by the mercies of God'. The life of the Christian is a loving response to God's mercy, which was shown on so many occasions in the past but has been revealed above all in Jesus Christ, as Paul has richly illustrated earlier in the letter. Christians are to 'present their bodies as a living sacrifice'. The offering of animal sacrifice in the temple has given way to the self-offering of the human person. It is this sacrifice which is now 'holy and acceptable to God'.

This for Paul is 'your spiritual worship'. The Greek word used here and translated in the NRSV as 'spiritual' is *logikos*. This phrase means more precisely 'your worship according to your rational mind'. Those who know and trust in Christ logically no longer offer animal sacrifice, but the sacrifice of their own lives. This new worship takes the place of the old.

v.2 Paul tells the Romans not to be conformed to 'this world' or 'this age'. The Greek word *aion* refers primarily to a period of time, or 'an age'. It is the Greek equivalent of the Latin word *saeculum*. 1 Peter 1:14 says, in similar fashion: 'do not be conformed to the desires that you formerly had in ignorance'. The essential is that the Christian should live according to his new faith, his new mind. The Fourth Gospel and the First Letter of John use the Greek word *kosmos*, 'the world', to speak in similar fashion of what is not in conformity to faith.

By contrast the Christian should 'be transformed by the renewing of the mind (Greek *nous*)'. This transformation uses the Greek term *metamorphoo*, which Paul uses in 2 Corinthians 3:18: 'all of us are being transformed into the same image from one degree of glory to another'. Here Paul does not speak of an image but of a process involving a new mind, the mind of those who believe in Christ. It is a call to radical renewal and to rejection of the world's wisdom. In 1 Corinthians 2:15 Paul says of believers: 'We have the mind (Greek *nous*) of Christ'.

St John Chrysostom comments:

How is the body to become a sacrifice? Let the eye look on no evil thing, and it has already become a sacrifice. Let the tongue say nothing filthy, and it has become an offering. Let your hand do nothing evil, and it has become a whole burnt offering. But even this is not enough, for we must have good works also. The hand must do alms, the mouth must bless those who curse it, and the ears must find time to listen to the reading of Scripture. Sacrifice allows of no unclean thing. It is the first fruits of all other actions. (Homilies on Romans 20)

This change of mind enables Christians to make true judgements about God's will. They can confidently discern what is 'good, acceptable and perfect'.

Gifts that Differ

v.3 Paul urges the Roman Christians not to overestimate their own worth. Paul uses three verbs having the Greek root *phronein*, which means 'to think'. He tells them not to 'think more highly' (Greek *huperphronein*) of themselves than they ought to 'think' (Greek *phronein*), but to 'think soberly' (Greek *sophronein*). The final form *sophronein* is related to the virtue of moderation, denoted by the Greek word *sophrosune*.

God, says Paul, has assigned a 'measure of faith' to each. This is perhaps a first allusion to the gifts of God about which Paul will speak in the following verses. In Ephesians 4:7 we read: 'Each of us was given grace according to the measure of Christ's gift.'

vv.4-5 Just as the human body has many members with different functions, so in Christ the many members with different gifts are one body. This analogy of the body is found also in 1 Corinthians, but in this latter case Paul says Christians are 'the body of Christ', not simply as here 'one body in Christ'. Paul stresses the different gifts of different people but also that they belong together in community.

v.6 Different gifts, known as 'charisms' (Greek *charismata*), are now listed. People have these charisms according to the grace (Greek *charis*) given to them by God.

Paul lists seven charisms, indicating by the number seven the completeness of God's provision for the common good. The first of the seven charisms is 'prophecy', the gift of speaking in the name of God. Prophecy is prominent among the gifts enumerated by Paul in 1 Corinthians 12, in verses 10 and 28. Here Paul instructs the Romans that prophecy must be exercised 'in proportion to faith'. The literal rendering of this is 'according to the analogy of faith'.

The word sophronein *is also used in the gospels of the healing of demoniacs, which results in them being 'in their right mind'.*

Mark 5:15 They came to Jesus and saw the demoniac sitting there, clothed and in his right mind.

Luke 8:35 People came out to see what had happened, and when they came to Jesus, they found the man from whom the demons had gone sitting at the feet of Jesus, clothed and in his right mind.

1 Corinthians 12:12 For just as the body is one and has many members, and all the members of the body, though many, are one body, so it is with Christ.

1 Corinthians 12:27 Now you are the body of Christ and individually members of it.

This phrase has a long history in the development of Christian theology. The 'analogy of faith' is the way the different truths of faith fit together. What is proclaimed in prophecy should never be in conflict with the basic tenets of the faith received.

v.7 The second charism is 'ministry' or 'service' (Greek *diakonia*). This is of course a wide-ranging term which covers all kind of activity. Later in the letter Paul will use the word *diakonia* of his bringing financial assistance to the Christians in Jerusalem, the collection which he has taken up in the churches of Macedonia and Achaia. In Romans 15:31 Paul expresses the prayer that his 'service' may be acceptable to the saints in Jerusalem. The third charism is 'teaching'. The Greek word *didaskalia* becomes synonymous not only with the activity of Christian teaching but also with its content. It is used in the latter sense in 1 Timothy 1:10, where Timothy is urged to avoid whatever is 'contrary to sound teaching'.

v.8 A further four charisms are listed in this verse. The 'exhorter' (Greek *ho parakalon*) may be one who gives consolation and encouragement to members of the community in time of need. In 1 Thessalonians 5:11 Paul gives similar advice to all members of the community: 'Encourage one another and build up each other, as indeed you are doing.' The fifth charism concerns the sharing of wealth. This should be practised in 'simplicity' (Greek *haplotes*). There should be no ulterior motive. The penultimate charism is that of the leader (Greek *ho proistamenos*), who is required to show diligence (Greek *spoude*). In 1 Thessalonians 5:12 Paul refers to those 'who have charge of you in the Lord'. Finally, there is the charism of the one who shows mercy, or compassion (Greek *ho eleon*), which must be exercised in cheerfulness and not grudgingly. There is a striking juxtaposition here of mercy and cheerfulness (Greek *hilarotes*), a word found only here in the New Testament.

Paul's Litany of Good Works

With verse 9 there begins an extraordinary list of good works and praiseworthy qualities, which are put down in an apparently random order, though some scholars have detected attempts to organise the material. Sometimes these exhortations come in contrasting pairs, as in the call in verse 15 to 'rejoice with those who rejoice, and weep with those who weep'. The grammar of these exhortations is extraordinarily loose. While translations into English unavoidably use imperatives, such as 'hate what is evil' (verse 9), the Greek original often uses adjectives, participles and infinitives, as well as the occasional imperative. For example 'hate what is evil' is in the original 'hating what is evil', and 'do not lag in zeal' in verse 11 is literally 'not lazy in zeal'.

vv.9-13 These initial verses concern relations within the Christian community. While in 1 Corinthians 13 Paul had spoken of *agape* as the greatest of the charisms, here he simply places it at the start of his litany. This self-giving love must be *anupokritos*. It must be totally sincere and lacking in hypocrisy. We can recall the constant accusation levelled at the Pharisees in Matthew chapter 23 of being 'hypocrites', wearing a mask of virtue and displaying a pretence of love. Love must be genuine.

Such love must be shown above all to those who are members of the Christian community. In verse 10 Paul uses the word *philadelphia*, literally 'love of the brothers and sisters', translated here as 'mutual affection'. *Philadelphia* is more specific than *agape*, since it refers to love within the community.

In verse 11 the reference to 'the spirit' is surely to the 'Spirit of life in Christ Jesus', of which Paul spoke at length in chapter 8. Being ardent in the Spirit is paired with serving the Lord. The exhortations concerning hope, patience in suffering, and perseverance in prayer in verse 12 echo Paul's teachings earlier in the letter, particularly in 5:2-4 and 8:26-27. Verse 13 speaks both of meeting the needs of those who belong to the community, the 'saints' (Greek *hagioi*), and of 'love

St John Chrysostom comments:
If you have love, you will not notice the loss of your money, the labour of your body, the toil of your words, your trouble or your ministering, but you will bear everything courageously. (Homilies on Romans 21)

In 1 Thessalonians 4:9-10 Paul wrote: Now concerning love of the brothers and sisters, you do not need to have anyone write to you, for you yourselves have been taught by God to love one another; and indeed you do love all the brothers and sisters throughout Macedonia.

of the stranger', in Greek *philoxenia*, a word used only here by Paul. Love shown within the local community is only a start. The community must welcome strangers.

vv.14-21 Paul proceeds with a first reference to those who are not well-disposed to Christians, 'those who persecute you' in verse 14. While verses 15-16 seem to lose this focus, it is recaptured in the following verses. The Christian behaviour encouraged here reflects the finest teaching of Jesus in Matthew's Sermon on the Mount and Luke's parallel material. The imperative 'bless' in verse 14 is found again in Luke 6:28: 'Bless those who curse you, pray for those who abuse you.'

The same theme continues in verse 17, where there is an echo of what Jesus says in the Sermon on the Mount in response to the saying 'An eye for an eye and a tooth for a tooth'. In Matthew 5:39 Jesus says: 'But I say to you, Do not resist an evildoer.'

The Christian attitude to hurt inflicted by others is considered further in the final verses. In verse 19 Paul calls his listeners 'beloved' (Greek *agapetoi*), a mode of address frequent in the First Letter of John. In 1:7 Paul had referred to the Roman Christians as 'beloved of God'. Paul seems to suggest that these beloved in Rome are called by their very nature to show *agape* to all, even to enemies. In verse 19 Paul quotes from Deuteronomy 32:35 to indicate that vengeance on evil is for God alone.

Verse 20 contains a quotation from Proverbs 25:21-22, and the love of enemies is again stressed. Heaping burning coals on an enemy's head is a confusing image, but the implication is clearly that love can change even the hardest heart. A similar proverb can be found in the 'Wisdom of Amenemope', an ancient Egyptian collection of wise sayings, traces of which are found in the Book of Proverbs.

The final imperatives in verse 21 are, unlike previous imperatives, in the singular and thus address each individual directly: 'do not be overcome by evil, but overcome evil with good'. The verse encapsulates what has been explained in the preceding verses.

The Wisdom of Amenemope was produced about 1200 BC. A papyrus manuscript of the work, which dates to about 600 BC, is kept in the British Museum. There are similarities between this Egyptian composition and the book of Proverbs. The following passage from the Egyptian work helps us to understand Proverbs 25:21-22 and consequently Romans 12:20: 'Fill the wicked man's belly with bread of your own, that he be sated and weep.'

St Jerome writes:

If someone does you a wrong and in return you do him good, you will be heaping coals of fire on his head. In other words, you are curing him of his vices and burning out his malice, in order to bring him to repentance. (Homilies on the Psalms 41)

Boat people in Lampedusa receive help.

The Word Lives On

The opening two verses of Romans 12 are read on the Twenty-Second Sunday in Ordinary Time in Year A as the second reading at Mass. On Tuesday of the thirty-first week in Year 1 Romans 12:5-16 is read as part of the four-week reading of Romans on weekdays. Romans 12:3-13 is also a possible reading for the celebration of the feasts of pastors, and Romans 12:9-16 is an alternative first reading on 31st May, the Feast of the Visitation of the Blessed Virgin Mary.

With their wide-ranging encouragement to Christian life these verses are also suitable for the celebration of the sacraments. Romans 12:4-8, which includes the section on the 'graces of state', is one of the possible readings for Holy Orders. An extensive reading from the chapter (verses *1-2* and *9-18*) is also among the New Testament readings for the celebration of marriage. 12:1-13 is among the readings possible for Religious Profession.

The Dogmatic Constitution on the Church of the Second Vatican Council states: All the disciples of Christ, persevering in prayer and praising God, should present themselves as a sacrifice, living, holy and pleasing to God. (Lumen Gentium 10)

Live the Word of God

Listen once more to the reading.

Suggestions for reflection and prayer

Paul invites the Romans to offer their bodies as a living sacrifice to God.

❖ How might I respond to this invitation in my daily life?

We are called to be transformed by the renewing of our minds.

❖ How do the media, advertising, and the values of the world impede this transformation?

❖ What obstacles do we ourselves put in the way of this renewal?

We are one body in Christ.

❖ To what extent do I value the gifts and promote the standing of other members of Christ's body?

❖ Am I jealous of the achievements and talents of others?

'Bless those who persecute you!'

❖ How well do I live up to the call of Jesus to pardon those who offend me and look after my enemies?

❖ Do I ever put 'burning coals' on the head of someone I dislike?

What connections are there between the teaching of Paul in this chapter and the teaching of Jesus in the gospels?

In his Encyclical Letter Veritatis Splendor of 1993 Blessed John Paul II wrote:

In the moral catechesis of the Apostles, besides exhortations and directions connected to specific historical and cultural situations, we find an ethical teaching with precise rules of behaviour. This is seen in their Letters, which contain the interpretation, made under the guidance of the Holy Spirit, of the Lord's precepts as they are to be lived in different cultural circumstances. (26)

Opposite: The Theological Virtues, Hope, Love and Faith.

The Duty of Love

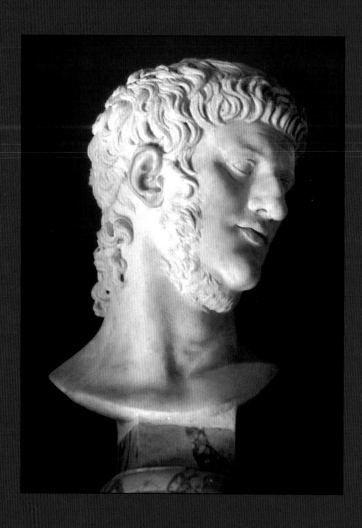

Hear the Word of God

Romans 13:1-14

Let every person be subject to the governing authorities; for there is no authority except from God, and those authorities that exist have been instituted by God. [2] Therefore whoever resists authority resists what God has appointed, and those who resist will incur judgement. [3] For rulers are not a terror to good conduct, but to bad. Do you wish to have no fear of the authority? Then do what is good, and you will receive its approval; [4] for it is God's servant for your good. But if you do what is wrong, you should be afraid, for the authority does not bear the sword in vain! It is the servant of God to execute wrath on the wrongdoer. [5] Therefore one must be subject, not only because of wrath but also because of conscience. [6] For the same reason you also pay taxes, for the authorities are God's servants, busy with this very thing. [7] Pay to all what is due to them - taxes to whom taxes are due, revenue to whom revenue is due, respect to whom respect is due, honour to whom honour is due.

[8] Owe no one anything, except to love one another; for the one who loves another has fulfilled the law. [9] The commandments, 'You shall not commit adultery; You shall not murder; You shall not steal; You shall not covet'; and any other commandment, are summed up in this word, 'Love your neighbour as yourself.' [10] Love does no wrong to a neighbour; therefore, love is the fulfilling of the law.

[11] Besides this, you know what time it is, how it is now the moment for you to wake from sleep. For salvation is nearer to us now than when we became believers; [12] the night is far gone, the day is near. Let us then lay aside the works of darkness and put on the armour of light; [13] let us live honourably as in the day, not in revelling and drunkenness, not in debauchery and licentiousness, not in quarrelling and jealousy. [14] Instead, put on the Lord Jesus Christ, and make no provision for the flesh, to gratify its desires.

Opposite: The Emperor Nero.

Understand the Word of God

This session will explore:

❖ the Christian attitude to the secular power

❖ love as the summary of the commandments

❖ readiness for the day

Setting in the Letter

After lengthy and complex chapters of teaching, Paul began in chapter 12 to consider the basic principles for living the Christian life. This chapter also included a long list of practical counsels. Exhortations about the practicalities of life continue in chapter 13, in which he deals with three specific issues. In the first section (verses 1-7) he gives advice about how Christians should relate to the secular power. In verses 8-10 Paul deals with the commandment to love as the fulfilment of the law. Finally, in verses 11-14, he gives advice on vigilance and preparedness for the return of Christ.

What Kind of Text?

The first section is remarkable in that it neither quotes from Scripture, nor does it refer explicitly or implicitly to Christ. For these reasons there are those who question whether verses 1-7 have been inserted into Paul's letter. Nevertheless, these verses deal with an issue of constant importance for people of faith at all times: what attitude should believers have to the secular power, particularly if the power in question does not share their beliefs?

At the time the Letter to the Romans was written, about the year 57, there was growing tension between the Jews and the Romans. In the Roman province of Palestine this would reach a climax with the Jewish Revolt against Rome in 66 AD, and the subsequent war which ended with the destruction of Jerusalem in the year 70.

Jews had been expelled from Rome in about the year 49 by the emperor Claudius because of the unrest among them, probably caused by rivalry between Jews and Jewish Christians, since Christianity was at this time seen as a sect within Judaism. The Jews had returned to Rome at the death of Claudius in 54.

The Roman writer Tacitus reports that at the time Paul wrote the Letter to the Romans there was considerable disquiet throughout the Empire over taxation and in particular over the collecting of taxes by those officials known as *publicani*. These would line their own pockets with the extra taxation they demanded from the people. In Luke 3:13 John the Baptist instructs the tax collectors: 'Collect no more than the amount prescribed for you.' The emperor Nero, who ruled from 54 until 68, even considered taking steps to ease the burden of taxation in order to gain popularity with the citizens. It is against this background that Paul gives advice about the paying of taxes.

Later in our text Paul goes on to consider love as the fulfilment of the law. This piece of teaching, unlike the previous one, includes quotations from Scripture. The final verses, on the imminence of salvation, reach their climax in verse 14 with the exhortation: 'Put on the Lord Jesus Christ.'

In the gospels tax-collectors like Zacchaeus (Luke 19) are presented alongside the sinners as needing the message of conversion brought by Jesus. The Greek term is telones and in Latin translations of the gospels they are called publicani, which gives us the English term 'publican', now used for those who run public houses.

Even later in the century, in a time of persecution, the First Letter of Peter urges respect for the civil authorities: For the Lord's sake accept the authority of every human institution, whether of the emperor as supreme, or of governors, as sent by him to punish those who do wrong and to praise those who do right. (1 Peter 2:13-14) Later, in 2:17, we read: Honour everyone. Love the family of believers. Fear God. Honour the emperor.

We read in the Catechism of the Catholic Church: Those subject to authority should regard those in authority as representatives of God, who has made them stewards of his gifts. Their loyal collaboration includes the right, and at times the duty, to voice their just criticisms of that which seems harmful to the dignity of persons and to the good of the community. (2238)

Commentary: verse by verse reading

Obedience to Civil Authorities

v.1 It is remarkable that Paul applies this teaching to every human being, and does not restrict it to Christians. He makes no connection with the teaching of Jesus, and there is a presumption that civil authorities always foster the common good. In an age when tyranny was widespread it is strange that the possibility of a tyrannical government is not considered by Paul. We can only speculate about the reason why Paul is so insistent that the Christians of Rome should be good citizens. Had he learnt of opposition by Christians to the Roman authorities and was he perhaps fearful of the consequences?

v.2 This verse is dominated by the idea of resisting authority. Paul in fact uses two different Greek words here *(antitasso* and *anthistemi)*. Both begin with the prefix *anti,* which means 'against'. To resist authority is to oppose 'what God has appointed'. The Greek term used here is *diatage*, which has the sense of the 'ordinance' or 'direction' which God has laid down. Those who resist authority oppose God and bring judgement on themselves. Paul seems to imply that such judgement will be exercised by the civil authority.

Relief depicting a tax collecting scene.

v.3 Paul insists that rulers will only punish those who do evil. Once again he does not consider the possibility of unjust rulers.

v.4 In a further development Paul twice refers to 'authority' as 'God's servant'. This may remind us of the way, in the Jewish Scriptures, individual rulers, even though pagan, were sometimes considered as servants of God. For Paul, the civil authority has the task of furthering the common good, and punishing evil doers by exercising God's wrath.

Jeremiah 27:6 God says: 'I have given all these lands into the hand of King Nebuchadnezzar of Babylon, my servant.'

Isaiah 44:28 God says of Cyrus: 'He is my shepherd, and he shall carry out all my purpose.'

v.5 Submission to lawful authority must not only be motivated by fear of punishment, what Paul describes as 'wrath', the 'anger of God' unleashed against the wicked first mentioned in Romans 1:18, but also by the promptings of conscience. The idea of conscience (Greek *suneidesis*), though unknown in the Old Testament, is frequently found in Greek philosophy and taken up by Paul to refer to the promptings of the heart inspired by the Spirit. In Romans 9:1, when he began considering the situation of the Jewish people, Paul spoke of how his conscience confirmed the truth of what he wrote 'by the Holy Spirit'. In 2 Corinthians 1:12 he writes: 'This is our boast, the testimony of our conscience: we have behaved in the world with frankness and godly sincerity, not by earthly wisdom but by the grace of God – and all the more toward you.'

vv.6-7 Paul now gives an example of such submission to civil authority: the paying of taxes. He makes a distinction between direct taxes (Greek *phoros*) and revenue charged on the exchange of goods (Greek *telos*). The collection of taxes is understood to be for the common good. Similarly, respect and honour are encouraged. While in the Christian community there should be no sense of rank or superiority, Christians should still show respect to those who are leaders in civil society.

Paul may well have known the teaching of Jesus recorded in Mark 12:17 (to which there are parallels in *Matthew 22:21* and *Luke 20:25*): 'Give to Caesar the things that are Caesar's, and to God the things that are God's.'

The Catechism of the Catholic Church teaches: Submission to authority and co-responsibility for the common good make it morally obligatory to pay taxes, to exercise the right to vote, and to defend one's country. (2240)

Love and the Law

v.8 In the previous verse Paul spoke about paying what is due (Greek *tas opheilas*). Now he speaks of owing (Greek *opheilete*) no one anything except the obligation of love. We are clearly back into the familiar territory of the moral teaching of Judaism and Christianity. Paul refers to love as a debt which has to be paid in an attempt to stress its essential presence in Christian life. He naturally uses the word *agapan,* which signifies self-giving love, rather than the lesser love expressed by *philein*, the love characteristic of friendship. There is a close similarity between Paul's use of words here and that found in 1 John 4:11: 'Beloved, since God loved us so much, we also ought (Greek *opheilomen*) to love (Greek *agapan*) one another.'

Paul has spoken already of the fulfilment of the law in 8:4, when he wrote about the 'just requirement of the law' being fulfilled in those who 'walk according to the Spirit'. Now he explains that it is by loving others that the law is 'fulfilled'. The idea of the 'fulfilment of the law' will return in verse 10.

v.9 Paul now quotes directly from the Decalogue, which is recorded in Exodus 20 and Deuteronomy 5. Perhaps surprisingly, the four commandments which he quotes in full all start with a negative. Each one in its own way forbids a particular way of hurting a neighbour. Paul then sums up all the commandments in the words of Leviticus 19:18, 'Love your neighbour as yourself.'

It is well known that the Pentateuch contains several law codes, collections of the ancient laws of Israel, some perhaps going back to the time of Moses, and others developed and codified in the following centuries. The Decalogue, or Ten Commandments, appears in Exodus 20 just before the collection of laws known as the 'Covenant Code'. The version found in Deuteronomy 5 has a few differences. For example, the justification for keeping the Sabbath holy in Exodus 20:11 is that God rested after the work of creation, while, in Deuteronomy 5:15, it is the memory of being slaves in Egypt. The quotation from Leviticus 19 comes from the 'Holiness Code'.

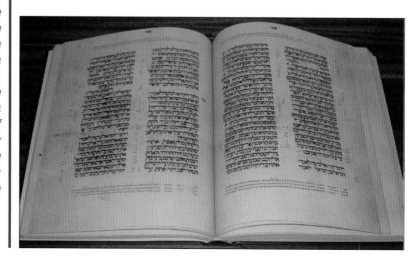

Hebrew Bible.

v.10 Love is the fulfilment (Greek to *pleroma*) of the law. In the Book of Wisdom we read: 'Love is the keeping (Greek *teresis*) of wisdom's laws' (*6:18*). Paul may well have been familiar with the story of Jesus' meeting with the scribe in Mark 12:28-34, and with Jesus' own summary of the law as love of God and love of neighbour.

Put on the Lord Jesus Christ!

v.11 Any command, and especially the commandment to love, takes on added urgency, because the time is near. Paul uses the word *kairos* of the expected and long-awaited time of salvation. This time has already arrived, and its final consummation is eagerly expected. He then uses the Greek word *hora,* which means the hour or moment. In writing of the hour for rising, or being roused, from sleep Paul uses the resurrection verb *egeirein*. In the parable of the wise and foolish virgins, the time of the Master's arrival is the time to rise up and be ready to accompany him (*Matthew 25:7*). Rising from sleep is an image of rising to the new life of the resurrection.

Salvation is closer than when we first believed. At the very start of the letter Paul had made the connection between faith and salvation by describing the gospel as 'the power of God for salvation to everyone who has faith' (*1:16*). In 10:10 Paul had written: 'One believes with the heart and so is justified, and one confesses with the mouth and so is saved.' For Paul, justification and salvation come through believing. Salvation is here described as 'nearer to us now'. Its fullness is still awaited but seemingly imminent.

v.12 The rich imagery of night and day is now introduced. The hours of night are almost over and there is need to be ready for the day. In 1 Thessalonians 5:5 Paul uses a similar image: 'You are all children of light and children of the day; we are not of the night or of darkness.' Paul is aware of the constant struggle to live as children of the light. The 'works of darkness' must be 'taken off' and replaced by the 'armour of light'. It is as if one type of clothing is to be replaced by another. The image of armour is found again in 1 Thessalonians 5:8, where Paul refers to 'the breastplate of faith and love, and for a helmet the hope of salvation'.

Mark 12:30-31: 'You shall love the Lord your God with all your heart, and with all your soul, and with all your mind, and with all your strength. You shall love your neighbour as yourself.'

Matthew 22:40 'On these two commandments hang all the law and the prophets.'

St John Chrysostom writes:

The day is calling us to get ready for the battle. Do not be afraid at the thought of bearing arms. It is a heavy and distasteful duty when we have to bear a visible suit of armour, but in this case it is desirable and worth it. For the arms we are called to bear are those of the light! (Homilies on Romans 24)

v.13 The first part of this verse would be more literally translated as: 'Let us walk decently.' The Greek word *euschemonos*, translated here as 'honourably', is found again in 1 Thessalonians 4:12, where Paul writes 'behave properly towards outsiders and be dependent on no one'. It has the sense of what is proper or decent. The sense emerges more clearly from the contrasting content of the rest of the verse, where behaviours which are improper and indecent are listed.

The first pair of words, 'revelling and drunkenness', are again found together in Galatians 5:21, in a long list of 'works of the flesh'. 'Debauchery' and 'licentiousness' refer to sexual immorality. The second of these terms is found in Galatians 5:19 in the same long list, and the final pair, 'quarrelling and jealousy', are found in Galatians 5:20.

v.14 Having given examples of activities to be discarded, Paul once again uses the image of putting on clothes, only this time he says: 'Put on the Lord Jesus Christ!' In Galatians 3:27 he writes: 'As many of you as were baptised into Christ have clothed yourselves with Christ.' Those baptised into Christ reject the desires of the flesh.

St Augustine of Hippo teaches:

Provision for the flesh is not to be condemned if it has to do with the needs of bodily health. But if it is a question of unnecessary delights or luxuries, a person who enjoys the delights of the flesh is rightly chastised. For in that case he makes provision for the desires of the flesh, and 'he who sows in the flesh will reap corruption in the flesh'. (On Romans 77)

Right: St Francis Renounces all Worldly Goods by Giotto di Bondone.

Opposite page: The Statue of St Paul in St Peter's Square.

The Word Lives On

Not surprisingly, perhaps owing to their rather secular content, the first seven verses of Romans chapter 13 never appear in the lectionary. Romans 13:8-10 is read on the Twenty-third Sunday in Ordinary Time in Year A as the second reading at Mass. On Wednesday of the thirty-first week in Year 1 the same verses are read as part of the four-week reading of Romans on weekdays. Romans 13:11-14, with its focus on vigilance and preparedness, is the second reading on the First Sunday of Advent in Year A.

Romans 13:13-14 is crucial to St Augustine's final decision to become a Christian, as he narrates in Book 8 of his 'Confessions':

'I was saying these things and weeping in the most bitter contrition of my heart, when suddenly I heard the voice of a boy or a girl I know not which, coming from the neighbouring house, chanting over and over again, "Take and read! Take and read!" Immediately I ceased weeping and began most earnestly to think whether it was usual for children in some kind of game to sing such a song, but I could not remember ever having heard the like. So, damming the torrent of my tears, I got to my feet, for I could not but think that this was a divine command to open the Bible and read the first passage I should light upon. For I had heard how Anthony, accidentally coming into church while the gospel was being read, received the admonition as if what was read had been addressed to him: "Go and sell what you have and give it to the poor, and you shall have treasure in heaven; and come and follow me." By such an oracle he was forthwith converted to thee.

'So I quickly returned to the bench where Alypius was sitting, for there I had put down the apostle's book when I had left there. I snatched it up, opened it, and in silence read the paragraph on which my eyes first fell: "Not in rioting and drunkenness, not in debauchery and licentiousness, not in strife and envying, but put on the Lord Jesus Christ, and make no provision for the flesh to gratify its desire." (*Rom 13:13-14*) I wanted to read no further, nor did I need to. For instantly, as the sentence ended, there was infused in my heart something like the light of full certainty and all the gloom of doubt vanished away.' (*Confessions VIII.29*)

Portrait of St Augustine by Justus van Gent.

Live the Word of God

Listen once more to the reading.

Suggestions for reflection and prayer

Paul teaches that everyone should be subject to the civil authorities.

❖ How should Christians behave when faced with unjust laws?

Consider the quotation from Pope John Paul II given on this page.

For Paul the commandment to love is central.

❖ How does the teaching of Paul compare with that of Jesus?

'Love is the fulfilling of the law.'

❖ Should Christians therefore obey all the injunctions of the Jewish law?

Paul calls the Romans to 'lay aside the works of darkness'.

❖ Is it possible that we need to do the same?

❖ What might 'putting on the Lord Jesus Christ' mean in your life?

Paul sends this moral teaching to a community he has never met.

❖ How do you think they reacted to it?

In his Encyclical Letter Evangelium Vitae *of 1995 Pope John Paul II tackled the problem of unjust laws:*

Abortion and euthanasia are crimes which no human law can claim to legitimise. There is no obligation in conscience to obey such laws; instead there is a grave and clear obligation to oppose them by conscientious objection. From the very beginnings of the Church, the apostolic preaching reminded Christians of their duty to obey legitimately constituted public authorities, but at the same time it firmly warned that 'we must obey God rather than men'. (73)

Augustine and Alypius by Benozzo Gozzoli.

Paul's Future Plans

Hear the Word of God

Romans 15:14-33

[14] I myself feel confident about you, my brothers and sisters, that you yourselves are full of goodness, filled with all knowledge, and able to instruct one another. [15] Nevertheless, on some points I have written to you rather boldly by way of reminder, because of the grace given me by God [16] to be a minister of Christ Jesus to the Gentiles in the priestly service of the gospel of God, so that the offering of the Gentiles may be acceptable, sanctified by the Holy Spirit. [17] In Christ Jesus, then, I have reason to boast of my work for God. [18] For I will not venture to speak of anything except what Christ has accomplished through me to win obedience from the Gentiles, by word and deed, [19] by the power of signs and wonders, by the power of the Spirit of God, so that from Jerusalem and as far around as Illyricum I have fully proclaimed the good news of Christ. [20] Thus I make it my ambition to proclaim the good news, not where Christ has already been named, so that I do not build on someone else's foundation, [21] but as it is written, 'Those who have never been told of him shall see, and those who have never heard of him shall understand.'

[22] This is the reason that I have so often been hindered from coming to you. [23] But now, with no further place for me in these regions, I desire, as I have for many years, to come to you [24] when I go to Spain. For I do hope to see you on my journey and to be sent on by you, once I have enjoyed your company for a little while. [25] At present, however, I am going to Jerusalem in a ministry to the saints; [26] for Macedonia and Achaia have been pleased to share their resources with the poor among the saints at Jerusalem. [27] They were pleased to do this, and indeed they owe it to them; for if the Gentiles have come to share in their spiritual blessings, they ought also to be of service to them in material things. [28] So, when I have completed this, and have delivered to them what has been collected, I will set out by way of you to Spain; [29] and I know that when I come to you, I will come in the fullness of the blessing of Christ.

[30] I appeal to you, brothers and sisters, by our Lord Jesus Christ and by the love of the Spirit, to join me in earnest prayer to God on my behalf, [31] that I may be rescued from the unbelievers in Judea, and that my ministry to Jerusalem may be acceptable to the saints, [32] so that by God's will I may come to you with joy and be refreshed in your company. [33] The God of peace be with all of you. Amen.

Opposite: Tarragona Amphitheatre.

Understand the Word of God

This session will explore:

- ❖ Paul's completed mission in the East
- ❖ his plans to travel to Rome, and then to Spain
- ❖ the collection for Christians in Jerusalem

Setting in the Letter

In these verses of chapter 15, the penultimate chapter of the letter, Paul addresses the Romans more personally. He has considered the moral implications of faith in Christ in chapters 12 to 14. In the final stages of this moral teaching he examines in 14:1 to 15:13 the specific situation of those he refers to as 'weak' (*14:1*).

Paul has in mind those who have not embraced the fullness of freedom brought by Christ and are excessively bound to ancient rules regarding food and drink, and the observance of holy days. They may well be Jewish Christian members of the Roman church. The 'strong' (*15:1*) are more likely to be Gentile Christians who were never bound by such laws. Paul's counsel is that those who are strong should never act in such a way as to offend the delicate consciences of the weak. There is a real need for forbearance. The strong should take Christ as their example, and not simply please themselves (*15:3*).

In Romans 15:14-33 Paul speaks of his future plans. Verse 33 contains a brief blessing, and, although this ending of the chapter is rather abrupt, there are some who consider that this might have been the original ending of the letter.

Chapter 16, with which the canonical text of Romans ends, may not be the original ending of the Letter to the Romans. In this chapter Paul addresses by name a lengthy list of Christians. Since Paul has never visited Rome, how is it that he is so familiar and friendly to so many individuals? It has often been suggested that chapter 16 might have been written for the Christians of another community, possibly

Ephesus, where Paul stayed for three years (*Acts 20:31*) and where he would have made many friends. Was chapter 16 perhaps attached to the Letter to the Romans when a copy of the letter was sent to Ephesus? Interestingly, one of the individuals mentioned is Epaenetus, who is described as 'the first convert in Asia for Christ' (*16:5*). Was Epaenetus from Ephesus, the capital of the Roman province of Asia?

What Kind of Text?

The kind of direct address found here is similar in tone to much of the opening chapter of Romans. Paul speaks with warmth to the Christian community in Rome and explains why he has written to them. He praises their goodness and knowledge (*15:14*), and expresses, as in 1:11, his deep desire to see them. He then explains why he plans first to go to Jerusalem and then to travel to Rome on his way to Spain.

The New Testament often speaks of the Roman province of 'Asia', which was in the western half of Asia Minor, the equivalent of modern Turkey:

Acts 19:10 All the residents of Asia, both Jews and Greeks, heard the word of the Lord.

1 Corinthians 16:19 The churches of Asia send greetings.

2 Corinthians 1:8 We do not want you to be unaware, brothers, of the affliction we experienced in Asia.

Revelation 1:4 John to the seven churches that are in Asia.

Library of Celsus, Ephesus.

Commentary: verse by verse reading

Paul's Missionary Strategy

The duty of Jewish priests was not simply to perform the temple sacrifices but also to deliver the word of God. The prophet Malachi (2:7) highlights the preaching role of the priests:

The lips of a priest should guard knowledge, and people should seek instruction from his mouth, for he is the messenger of the Lord of hosts.

In 1 Corinthians 9:16 Paul writes: If I proclaim the gospel this gives me no ground for boasting, for an obligation is laid on me, and woe to me if I do not proclaim the gospel!

v.14 Paul begins the conclusion of the letter with praise for those to whom he writes. The tone is similar to what he wrote in Romans 1:8: 'I thank my God through Jesus Christ for all of you, because your faith is proclaimed throughout the world.' Having praised their goodness (Greek *agathosune*) and knowledge (Greek *gnosis*), Paul refers to their readiness to admonish each other. In Acts 20:31, in his farewell speech to the elders of Ephesus, Paul is reported to have said: 'Therefore be alert, remembering that for three years I did not cease night or day to admonish everyone with tears.'

v.15 Paul excuses himself for writing sometimes in a forthright way by reminding the Romans that he has received a truly special grace.

v.16 The grace received by Paul is to be a 'minister of Christ Jesus to the Gentiles'. Paul uses the Greek word *leitourgos*. The word means something like 'minister of worship', and is clearly related to the word 'liturgy'. In Romans 1:9 Paul had said that he worshipped God with his spirit 'by announcing the gospel of his Son'. Paul considers his preaching as a way of worshipping God. He can therefore speak of himself as performing a 'priestly service' as he preaches the gospel of God. Through his preaching he brings a new offering to God, the offering of Gentiles who have been made holy through the Holy Spirit. Paul thus performs the two priestly duties of preaching and of making offerings to God.

v.17 Paul is ready to boast of the work he has done for God in Christ Jesus, and not of his own accomplishments. Paul has previously urged the Romans not to boast of their own achievements but of the salvation freely given to them by Christ. In Romans 3:27 Paul had written: 'Then what becomes of boasting? It is excluded.' In Romans 5:11, however, we read: 'We boast in God through our Lord Jesus Christ, through whom we have now received reconciliation.'

vv.18-19 Paul now qualifies his 'work for God' by describing it as 'what Christ has accomplished through me'. It is Christ who has brought about the obedience of the Gentiles. It has been accomplished by word and deed, even by signs and wonders, but all by the power of the Spirit. We have some knowledge of acts of healing worked by Paul from the Acts of the Apostles. Perhaps, in his reference to 'signs and wonders' here, Paul is more interested in the power of the Spirit in transforming people's lives than in miraculous healings.

Paul considers that his work in the East has reached completion. He traces an arc from Jerusalem to Illyricum to encompass the lands he has evangelised and to include his whole ministry in Syria, Asia Minor and modern-day Greece. Jerusalem he considers the starting point of his ministry, even though his call occurred near Damascus (*Galatians 1:17*). His preaching reflects the Church's mission, which moves out from Jerusalem, Judaea and Samaria 'to the ends of the earth' (*Acts 1:8*). Illyricum lies to the north of Macedonia and borders on the Adriatic Sea. Paul is implying that Italy and Spain are now in his sights.

v.20 Paul now explains his guiding principle for preaching. It is his intention to preach in those places where Christ has not yet been 'named'. Paul's words also point to the honour he feels at preaching where no Christian preacher has previously been heard. He is unwilling to build on someone else's foundation. In 1 Corinthians 3:5-9 Paul explains that both he and Apollos were making different contributions to the growth of the church in Corinth, but that the fundamental work was that of God. Paul has obvious talents for leadership in mission and the founding of new communities, but he is also able to work with others.

v.21 Paul introduces a text from Scripture to emphasise his mission to those who have not yet heard of Christ. Isaiah 52:15 comes early in the Fourth Song of the Servant (*Isaiah 52:13-53:12*). A message as yet unheard is about to be proclaimed. In Romans 10:16 Paul quoted another early verse of the song, Isaiah 53:1. The whole song was soon understood by Christians as referring to the saving death of Christ.

In Acts 14:8-10 there is an account of the healing of a cripple in Lystra, and in Acts 28:8-9 the healing from fever of the father of Publius, a leading citizen of Malta, is followed by the healing of 'the rest of the people on the island'.

In his remarkable document on evangelisation in the modern world, issued in 1975, Pope Paul VI wrote:

To reveal Jesus Christ and his Gospel to those who do not know them has been, ever since the morning of Pentecost, the fundamental programme which the Church has taken on as received from her Founder. The whole of the New Testament bears witness to a privileged and in a sense exemplary moment of this missionary effort which will subsequently leave its mark on the whole history of the Church. (Evangelii Nuntiandi 51)

vv.22-23 Paul has now explained why there has been such a delay in his visiting Rome. There are echoes here of Romans 1:10-11, where he described his enduring desire to visit them.

v.24 For the first time in the letter Paul mentions Spain. The Iberian peninsula was the western-most part of the Roman Empire. Having completed his work in the East he now intends to travel west, to new areas where Christ has not yet been 'named'. We do not know for certain whether there were Jewish communities in Spain at this time. While Jews from as far afield as Libya, Cyrene and Rome are named among the pilgrims coming to Jerusalem for the feast of Pentecost in Acts 2:10, there is no mention of Spain.

Paul's reason for visiting Rome now becomes clear. He is not intending to found a community, for the Roman church is already well established. In addition to strengthening their faith and being strengthened by them (*1:11-12*), Paul wishes to be 'sent on' by the Christians of Rome to his new mission in Spain. This surely means to be supported by their encouragement and prayers, and maybe also by some kind of monetary contribution.

The expression to be 'sent on' (Greek *propempein*) is found elsewhere in the New Testament, and in the Third Letter of John verses 6-8 there is this interesting passage: 'You will do well to send these brothers on in a manner worthy of God; for they began their journey for the sake of Christ, accepting no support from the Gentiles. Therefore we ought to support such people, so that we may become co-workers with the truth.' This letter is addressed to the Christian Gaius, who is commended for his support of the missionaries who have visited him. He has thus become a 'co-worker with the truth'. It is in the context of established Christian communities providing support for missionaries in their work of spreading the gospel that we can understand Paul's words in verse 24.

The Ministry to the Saints in Jerusalem

v.25 Before he visits Rome Paul must make a journey to Jerusalem. The collection to support poor Christians in Jerusalem is mentioned for the first time in Romans in this verse, but we find more information about it in others letters of Paul. In 1 Corinthians 16:1-4 we read: 'Now concerning the collection for the saints: you should follow the directions I gave to the churches of Galatia. On the first day of every week, each of you is to put aside and save whatever extra you earn, so that collections need not be taken when I come. And when I arrive, I will send any whom you approve with letters to take your gift to Jerusalem. If it seems advisable that I should go also, they will accompany me.'

In the second letter to the Corinthians Paul speaks more extensively about the collection. He urges the Christians of Corinth to imitate the generosity of the Lord Jesus: 'though he was rich, yet for your sakes he became poor' (*2 Corinthians 8:9*). In chapter 9 Paul encourages the Corinthians to remain faithful to their commitment to the poor.

v.26 Paul's references to Macedonia and Achaia confirm to the Christians of Rome that the churches of places like Philippi and Thessalonica, which lie in Macedonia, and Corinth, the capital of Achaia, have indeed contributed generously to the collection for the poor of Jerusalem. The phrase 'to share their resources' is literally 'to make community' (Greek *poiein koinonian*). Another early expression of such Christian solidarity is found in Acts 11:29, when the Christians of Syrian Antioch send aid 'to the brothers living in Judaea' at a time of famine.

Pope Paul VI writes: It is impossible to accept that in evangelisation one could or should ignore the importance of the problems so much discussed today, concerning justice, liberation, development and peace in the world. This would be to forget the lesson which comes to us from the Gospel concerning love of our neighbour who is suffering and in need. (Evangelii Nuntiandi 31)

v.27 Paul repeats what he said in the preceding verse that the Christians of Macedonia and Achaia 'were pleased' to make their contributions. In this way he stresses the freedom of their donations. Paul then curiously says that 'they owe it to them'. The Gentile Christians owe a debt to the Jewish Christians of Jerusalem in the sense that it was from the mother church in Jerusalem that the gospel originated. Since the Gentile churches have shared in the spiritual gifts of the church of Jerusalem, it is proper that they repay the debt they owe by sharing their material gifts with the poor of Jerusalem. We may recall that in 1:14 Paul spoke of himself as 'in debt' to the Gentiles. As apostle to the Gentiles, Paul had received a gift so great that he had to share it with others.

Underlying his work to bring material assistance to the Christians of Jerusalem lies Paul's profound awareness that all Christians, whether Jew or Gentile, are the one church of Christ. The sharing of material goods will help to heal any divisions between Christians of Jewish and Gentile origin.

vv.28-29 Paul restates his intention that, once the collection is delivered, he will set out for Rome and for Spain. When our translation says 'when I have delivered to them what has been collected' the literal meaning is 'when I have sealed for them this fruit'. Paul seems to be using an agricultural metaphor. When a tenant farmer delivered the harvested fruit to the owner of the land he farmed, the sacks of produce would be sealed with the farmer's seal to ensure he was properly remunerated. Paul seems to mean that the 'fruit' of the collection among the Gentile churches will be reliably entrusted by him in person to those for whom it was intended. Given both the difficulties in raising the collection, and the dangers of travelling with large amounts of money, this would be a real achievement. But the overriding importance of the collection is as an expression of solidarity and unity among Christians of different origins.

v.30 Paul began his more practical teaching about living the Christian life in Romans in 12:1 with the words 'I appeal to you, brothers.' He introduces these verses with the same words, as he speaks specifically about the particular trials he faces in the days ahead. What he asks for now is that the Christians in Rome 'struggle with me in prayer for me'. This is the literal meaning of what is translated here as 'join me in earnest prayer on my behalf'. Paul is deeply aware of the difficulties he will face as he travels to Jerusalem.

The Greek term *sunagonisasthai* has at its centre the word *agon*, which means 'struggle' or 'fight'. We find this image elsewhere too. In Colossians 1:29 Paul writes: 'I toil and struggle with all the energy that

Christ powerfully inspires within me.' A closer parallel to the present text is found in Colossians 4:12, where Paul says that Epaphras 'is always wrestling in his prayers on your behalf, so that you may stand mature and fully assured in everything that God wills'. In our text Paul invites the Romans to 'wrestle' or 'struggle' in their prayers for him.

v.31 This verse gives two intentions for prayer. The first is that Paul be 'rescued from the unbelievers in Judea'. This seems to refer to Jews who had known Paul but had never accepted faith in Christ and were consequently hostile to Paul. Paul might also have been anxious about those Jews who had become Christians but opposed the gospel he preached, which in their opinion disregarded the Law.

The second intention of prayer is that Paul's 'ministry (Greek *diakonia*) to Jerusalem may be acceptable to the saints'. Paul is worried that, due to misunderstanding of his preaching, the act of solidarity of the Gentile churches for the poor in Jerusalem might be rejected. In Acts 24:17 Paul informs the Roman governor Felix: 'Now after some years I came to bring alms to my nation and to offer sacrifices.' This seems to suggest that the collection was indeed accepted.

v.32 If all goes well, and if it is God's will, Paul is confident that he will then proceed on his journey to Rome. In the event, he will travel to Rome in custody, having appealed to be judged by the emperor in the face of the accusations made against him (*Acts 25:11*).

v.33 The chapter ends with a brief concluding blessing, which might in fact have been the ending of the whole letter. The Letter to the Galatians ends in a similarly brief way: 'May the grace of our Lord Jesus Christ be with your spirit, brothers.' (*6:18*)

In Acts 21 we are told that James, the leader of the Jerusalem church, informs Paul about the concerns of Jewish Christians who are 'zealous for the law' (21:20). Paul undergoes a rite of purification in the temple in order to allay their suspicions about him (21:26). Despite this, as the chapter continues, Paul faces considerable violence, and has to be rescued by Roman soldiers (21:31-33). It seems that Paul's fears expressed to the Christians of Rome were justified.

The Letter to the Romans as a whole ends with this prayer:

Now to God who is able to strengthen you according to my gospel and the proclamation of Jesus Christ, according to the revelation of the mystery that was kept secret for long ages but is now disclosed, and through the prophetic writings is made known to all the Gentiles, according to the command of the eternal God, to bring about the obedience of faith — to the only wise God, through Jesus Christ be the glory for ever! Amen. (16:25-27)

The Word Lives On

On Friday of the thirty-first week in Year 1 Romans 15:14-21 is read. The reading of selected verses from chapter 16 on the following day brings to an end the four-week reading of Romans on weekdays. No part of our text appears in the lectionary for Sundays. The final verses of the whole letter, 16:25-27, are read on the Fourth Sunday of Advent in Year A.

Pope Paul VI (1963-1978).

Live the Word of God

Listen once more to the reading.

Suggestions for reflection and prayer

Paul considers his work of preaching a 'priestly service' for God.

❖ What daily offerings are we called to make as members of God's priestly people?

Paul's primary duty is to proclaim the good news to those who do not know Christ.

❖ How can we make Christ known and understood by those who have not known him?

As he completes his preaching in the East, Paul is already intent on reaching Spain and proclaiming the good news there.

❖ How should we imitate his perseverance in the Christian vocation?

The collection for the poor in Jerusalem is an early example of Christian solidarity and strengthens the bonds between Jewish and Gentile Christians.

❖ How can Christians today take forward the work of peace and development?

The Letter to the Romans is a fascinating and challenging piece of writing.

❖ What will you take away with you from your reading of Romans?

❖ What points in Paul's teaching have most nourished your life of faith?

❖ What points will you need to revisit in this difficult letter?

Pope Paul VI gives this encouragement:

Let us therefore preserve our fervour of spirit. Let us preserve the delightful and comforting joy of evangelising, even when it is in tears that we must sow. May it mean for us – as it did for John the Baptist, for Peter and Paul, for the other Apostles and for a multitude of splendid evangelisers all through the Church's history – an interior enthusiasm that nobody and nothing can quench. May it be the great joy of our consecrated lives. And may the world of our time, which is searching, sometimes with anguish, sometimes with hope, be enabled to receive the Good News not from evangelisers who are dejected, discouraged, impatient or anxious, but from ministers of the Gospel whose lives glow with fervour, who have first received the joy of Christ, and who are willing to risk their lives so that the Kingdom may be proclaimed and the Church established in the midst of the world. (Evangelii Nuntiandi 80)

Picture Credits

P.1   St Paul by Marek Czarnecki. ©seraphicrestorations.com.

P.9   The Apostles St Peter and St Paul, El Greco, ©The Bridgeman Art Library .

P.11   Page with text of Epistle to the Romans 1:1-7, Oxyrhynchus 209, manuscript of the New Testament, designated by P10 on the list Gregory-Aland. Photo: Wikipedia.

P.12   Posting a letter. © Frederick Sneddon | Dreamstime.com.

P.15   Roman Emperor Claudius. Photo: Wikipedia.

P.18   Scales. ©2011 Photos.com, a division of Getty Images. All rights reserved.

P.19   Habakkuk by Donato di Niccolo di Betto Bardi Donatello. ©Photo Scala, Florence.

P.20   The Dream of St Joseph by Rembrandt Harmenszoon van Rijn. ©Interfoto / The Bridgeman Art Library.

P.21   Missionary Journeys of St Paul. ©Google.

P.21   Martin Luther. ©Google.

P.22   Melchisedek offering bread and wine to Abraham, Nave Mosaic, Santa Maria Maggiore, Rome. Photo © 2010 Holly Hayes/Art History Images. All rights reserved.

P.25   The Sacrifice of Abraham by Laurent de la Hire. ©2011 Photos.com, a division of Getty Images. All rights reserved.

P.28   Jews Praying in the Synagogue on Yom Kippur by Maurycy Gottlieb. Photo: Wikipedia.

P.31   Christ the Redeemer, Rio de Janeiro, Brazil. ©www.sxc.hu.

P.32   Man reading a Bible. ©www.sxc.hu.

P.33   St Therese. ©Alive Publishing.

P.34   Creation of Adam (detail from the Sistine Chapel) by Michelangelo. © 2011 License-Free Religious Art Image

P.37   Adam and Eve Expelled from the Garden of Eden. © 011 Photos.com, a division of Getty Images. All rights reserved.

P.41   Fol.126rb Christ enters Hell to rescue Adam and Eve and all the Just), Italian School, ©Biblioteca Reale, Turin, Italy / Alinari / The Bridgeman Art Library

P.43   John Henry Newman, by Sir John Everett Millais. ©Alive Publishing.

P.44   Adam by Antonio Rizzo. ©Photo Scala, Florence.

P.45   Adam and Eve. ©Oxlock/Dreamstime.com

P.46   Baptismal font in the ruins of the Church of St Mary, Ephesus, Turkey. ©Richard Goodrich/Dreamstime.com

P.49   Baby boy baptised. ©2011 Photos.com, a division of Getty Images. All rights reserved.

P.106   Mosaic of the dome (Saint Paul), Baptistery of the Arians, Ravenna, Italy. ©Photo Scala, Florence - courtesy of the Ministero Beni e Att. Culturali.

P.108   Pressing dough. ©Peter Galbraith/www.sxc.hu.

P.109   Ancient olive in Ortumannu, Sardinia. ©Patrizio Martorana/www.sxc.hu.

P.113   Olive branch. ©Stephanie Berghaeuser/www.sxc.hu.

P.114   Jeremiah, as depicted by Michelangelo from the Sistine Chapel ceiling. Image: Wikipedia.

P.115   Burial Site of St Paul, San Paolo fuori le Mura, Rome. ©Sacred Destinations.

P.116   St Paul the Apostle who took the Christian message to the Gentiles. ©Ann Ronan/Heritage Images/Scala, Florence.

P.118   Ss Peter and Paul Embracing (mosaic), Byzantine School, (12th century) / Duomo, Monreale, Sicily, Italy / Giraudon / The Bridgeman Art Library.

P.121   Christian agape, detail from sarcophagus lid, Museo Nazionale Romano. ©Photo Scala, Florence - courtesy of the Ministero Beni e Att. Culturali.

P.127   Boat people in Lampedusa ©PA Photos.

P.128   Hope, Charity, and Faith by Burne-Jones, St Martin's Church, Brampton, Cumbria.

P.130   Marble bust of Nero. ©2011 Photos.com, a division of Getty Images. All rights reserved.

P.132   Pound coins. ©2011 Photos.com, a division of Getty Images. All rights reserved.

P.134   Relief depicting a tax collecting scene, Gallo-Roman. ©Rheinisches Landesmuseum, Trier, Germany/ Giraudon/The Bridgeman Art Library.

P.136   Hebrew Bible. ©Asafesh/www.sxc.hu.

P.138   Scenes from the Life of Saint Francis: the Renunciation of Worldly Goods by Giotto di Bondone, San Francesco, Upper Church, Assisi, Italy / Giraudon / © The Bridgeman Art Library

P.139   The Statue of St Paul in St Peter's Square - Vatican City State. ©Sean Beldon/ iStockphoto.com.

P.140   Portrait of St Augustine by Justus van Gent. ©2011 Photos.com, a division of Getty Images. All rights reserved.

P.141   Episodes from the Life of St Augustine by Benozzo di Lese di Sandro Gozzoli. ©Sant' Agostino, San Gimignano, Italy / The Bridgeman Art Library.

P.142   Tarragona Amphitheatre, Photo: Bernard Gagnon.

P.145   Library of Celaus, Ephesus. ©Owen Tosh/www.sxc.hu.

P.151   Collection plate.

P.152   Pope Paul VI. Photo: Vatican City (picture official of Pope).

The Gospel of Matthew
Written by Henry Wansbrough
Edited by Adrian Graffy

The Gospel of Matthew presents Jesus to us as the great teacher, who in the Sermon on the Mount and his other speeches offers new teaching to a new community drawn from Jews and Gentiles. The disciples are instructed to bring the good news to all the nations of the earth. This gospel of the Church has much to offer us today.

UK:...............£9.99
Europe:......€12.50
Code:........278052

The Gospel of Mark
Written and edited by Adrian Graffy

The Gospel of Mark presents Jesus to us in a fresh and exciting way. In it Jesus throws down the challenge of discipleship. That same call to generosity of spirit and fidelity amid trials, the challenge to live by the gospel, is always before us.

UK:...............£9.99
Europe:......€12.50
Code:........278045

The Gospel of Luke
Written by Ian Boxall
Edited by Adrian Graffy

The Gospel of Luke invites us to embark on a journey of faith and discovery. This journey began when Jesus travelled from Galilee to Jerusalem, and continued in the Acts of the Apostles with the journeys of Philip, Peter, Barnabas and Paul. Our own journey of faith is part of this bigger journey, and Luke introduces us to fellow-travellers along the way.

UK:...............£9.99
Europe:......€12.50
Code:........278069

The Gospel of John
Written by john J Henry
Edited by Adrian Graffy

The Gospel of John is unique among the four gospels. It has been prized by many since early times as a valued source of spiritual nourishment. John's gospel interweaves the easily-grasped world of what is visible and material with the deeper world of reflection, mystery, and the Spirit. Its mystery, timelessness, and freshness constantly surprise us.

UK:...............£9.99
Europe:......€12.50
Code:........278076

The Acts of the Apostles
Written by Henry Wansbrough
Edited by Adrian Graffy

The Acts of the Apostles invites the reader to consider the early history of the Church and the outreach of the gospel 'from Jerusalem to Judea and Samaria and to the ends of the earth'. It is the story of the Holy Spirit guiding the Church from the beginning in the work of the gospel, which continues into our own time.

UK:...............£9.99
urope:......€12.50
de:........278120

The Gospels Box Set

This box set contains *The Gospel of Matthew*, *The Gospel of Mark*, *The Gospel of Luke* and *The Gospel of John*. A perfect resource for parishes, schools and individuals who wish to mine and plumb ever more deeply the riches and treasure of the Gospels.

UK:............£35.00
Europe:......€45.00
Code:........278083

To order, call our credit card HOTLINE: **+44 (0)1782 745600**
R visit: **www.alivepublishing.co.uk** OR email: **booksales@alivepublishing.co.uk**

Notes

Notes